108 Investment Mantras

Subhash Lakhotia
Tax Guru: CNBC Awaaz
Income Tax & Investment Consultant
Thinker, Motivator & Popular Public Speaker

DIAMOND BOOKS
www.diamondbook.in

Publisher : **Diamond Pocket Books (P) Ltd.**
X-30, Okhla Industrial Area, Phase-II
New Delhi-110020
Phone : 011-40712100, 41611861
Fax : 011-41611866
E-mail : sales@dpb.in
Website : www.diamondbook.in
Edition: 2015 (Revised)
Printed by : Repro Knowledgecast Limited, Thane

108 Investment Mantras
By - Subhash Lakhotia

The book is dedicated to my father
Shri R.N. Lakhotia
with whom I have been practicising
the investment mantras for
the last over 45 years and
still the journey goes on.

Preface

One of the most popular reality show on the T.V. screen before three years was the Bigg Boss show of Amitabh Bachhan on the Colors Channel. All those big artists who would be moving out from the said Bigg Boss home would then come up in another TV show hosted by me which was known as the Big M Show on CNBC Awaaz. While hosting this show I presented to these artists mainly from the Bollywood world my tips and ideas relating to investments. It is at that time I got the idea to write a small book for the benefit of the investors and to provide them various tips for smooth investment which would benefit them for years to come.

I am very happy to present this small little book for the benefit of all the investors of India. I am very confident that all the investors from 20 to 85 age-groups would surely benefit from these investment mantras. These investment mantras would result into money making ideas not merely for the reader but for his whole family as also for friends and relatives. I am happy that the first edition of the book was appreciated by the investors; hence I take pleasure in presenting this revised edition of the book for the benefit of investors.

I am thankful to my friend Shri N.K. Verma, the Chairman of Diamond Books for taking all the pains to publish this revised edition of the book in such a short time.

The book would be found to be of great help and utility to all persons who are looking for guidance relating to their investment strategy.

– Subhash Lakhotia

21-08-2015
Lakhotia Niwas
S-228, Greater Kailash Part-2
New Delhi -110048
Ph. 9810001665, 011-29215434
slakhotia@satyam.net.in

Know the Author
Mr. Subhash Lakhotia

Mr. Subhash Lakhotia is the Director of R.N. Lakhotia & Associates LLP. He is an Income-tax Practitioner for the last over 45 years. He regularly writes in various national dailies. He is the Director of **Lakhotia College of Taxation & Management.** He is practicing as a consultant on tax planning, tax documentation and investment planning. He has also addressed a number of seminars and lecture meetings on taxation and tax planning and is conducting the popular course known as 'Zero to Hero in Direct Taxes'.

He was selected as the best youth of India by the Lions International to represent India at the World Youth Congress held at Atlantic City, USA in 1970. He is Secretary General of Investors Club and President of Spiritual Club International and Unite to Invest (UTI). He is Chief

Strategist of Real Estate Strategy group and is actively associated with various professional bodies connected with real estate. He has written books on Income-tax, Investment, Real Estate and Spirituality. He is actively associated with Lions Clubs International. He has been awarded the "Sahityashree" award and "The Suryadatta National Award, 2010". In the year 2014 he was awarded the "Ambassador of Good Will" award by the International Association of Lions Clubs, USA.

Mr. Subhash Lakhotia is conducting a very popular show "Tax Guru" on every Wednesday, Saturday and Sunday on "CNBC AWAAZ" a popular TV Channel from house of CNBC. Recently the 500th episode of Tax Guru was aired on the TV Channel. The National Television Award, 2010 for "Best Business Talk Show of the Year" has been awarded to the tax Guru programme. He has instituted "Subhash Lakhotia Shrawan Kumar Puruskar" of Rs. 1 lakh per year and another award known as "Subhash Lakhotia Sewa Puruskar" also of Rs. 1 Lakh per annum.

Mailing Address: Date of Birth
Mr. Subhash Lakhotia 23.11.1949
Tax & Investment Consultant
S-228, Greater Kailash Part-2, New Delhi-110048
Phone: 011-29215434, 29215420, ***M.:*** 9810001665
E-mail: lakhotia49@gmail.com and thelakhotia@gmail.com

Contents

1

Investment in Sukanya Samriddhi Yojna – A Unique Scheme for Young Girl Child

For the prosperity of the girl child in particular a new scheme has been launched by the Government which is known as Sukanya Samriddhi Yojna. The basic aim of this scheme is to provide for education of the giri child and also to help in the marriage of the girl child. As a part of 'Beti Bachao Beti Padhao' Programme of the Prime Minister this scheme has been started. The scheme has been notified by Ministry of Finance vide Notification No. G.S.R. 863(E) dated 02.12.2014. Scheme becomes operational by notification of rules namely 'Sukanya Samriddhi Account Rules, 2014. Although the scheme has been announced towards the end of December 2014, certain tax concessions have been granted as per the Union Budget 2015-16. Under the scheme an account in the name of the girl child can be opened either with any Post Office in India doing the Savings Bank Account work or the account can also be opened with any branch of a commercial bank authorized by the Central Government to open the account under these rules. The scheme provides that the account may be opened by the natural or legal guardian in the name of a girl child from the birth of the girl child till she attains the age of ten years and any girl child, who had attained the age of ten years, one year prior to the commencement of these rules, shall also be eligible for opening of the account under these rules. It is also provided in the scheme that the account may be opened and operated upon in the name of the girl child and that it is further provi9ded that only one account may be opened under the above scheme for one girl child.

For the purpose of opening of the bank account the Birth certificate of a girl child in whose name the account is opened shall be submitted by the guardian at the time of opening of the account in post office or bank along with other documents relation to identity and residence proof of the depositor.

The scheme further provides that the account may be opened with an initial deposit of one thousand rupees and thereafter any amount in multiple of one hundred rupees may be deposited subject to the condition that a minimum of one thousand rupees shall be deposited in a financial year but the total money deposited in an account on a single occasion or in multiple occasions shall not exceed one lakh fifty thousand rupees in a financial year.

The deposits which are made in the name of the girl child may be made till completion of fourteen years from the date of opening the bank account in the above scheme.

The above mentioned account shall be operated by the natural or real guardian of the girl child till she attains the age of ten years. On attaining age of ten years, the account holder that the girl child herself operate the account, however, deposit in the account may be made by the guardian or any other person or authority. The scheme further provides that in the event of death of the account holder, the account shall be closed immediately on production of death certificate issued by the competent authority, and the balance at the credit of the account shall be paid along with interest till the months preceding the month of premature closure of the account, to the guardian of the account holder. The scheme further provides that the premature closure of the account may be affected only in cases of extreme compassionate grounds such as medical support in life threatening diseases, death, etc.

For the purpose of higher education and marriage of the girl child the scheme provides that to meet the financial requirement of the account holder withdrawal up to fifty per cent of the balance at the credit, at the end of preceding financial year shall be allowed. However, such withdrawal will be allowed only when the account holder the girl child attains the age of eighteen years.

The Sukanya Samriddhi Yojna furtherprovides that the account shall mature on completion of twenty one years from the date of opening of the account. It is also provided that where the marriage of the account holder takes place before completion of such period of twenty one years, the operation of the account shall not be permitted beyond the date of her marriage.

The amendments as proposed by the Finance Act, 2015 makes the investment in the above scheme interesting for your girl child. This is because the interest provided on the deposited amount will be at the rate of 9.1 per cent which will be tax free. Likewise, on investment in this scheme the person investing the money also enjoys deduction under section 80C within the overall limit of Rs. 1,50,000. Hence, for safeguarding the interest of the minor child the scheme apparently appears to be very good one.

❑❑❑

2

Investment in Tax Free Bonds

If you come in the highest income bracket – that to, if you have an income exceeding Rs. 10 lakh a year – surely it is worthwhile for you to make your investment in tax free bonds, especially if you calculate the impact of income-tax savings on the same. The investment in tax free bonds would be better than Bank Fixed Deposits. Grab fast the Tax Free Bonds, before they vanish.

Well, generally speaking the Tax Free Bonds are very good instruments for investment. They are safe and secured and no risk at all. There is no upper limit of investment in these Bonds. More details about these Bonds will be given after some time. But I would say that investment in Tax Free Bonds is very good option for investment by High Net Worth Individuals specially if they are compare with Bank FDR deposits because in respect of income from Bank Fixed Deposit income-tax payable is as high as 30 per cent whereas the interest income from these Bonds is completely tax free thereby the investor gets entire interest income tax free. All such persons who are coming within the higher income-tax bracket will be able to earn net higher interest after taking into consideration the impact of income-tax. The net extra yield would be about 1 per cent income comparing with Bank Fixed Deposit. Those coming in higher Income-tax Bracket may invest in these Bonds.

Now coming to other category of individuals I would say that individuals having income below Rs. 2,50,000 and generally making investment in Bank Fixed Deposit should not make investment of a single rupee in these Bonds because the net take home money for such individuals will be higher if these make investment in Bank Fixed Deposit. Next for such persons who have income up to Rs. 5,00,000 for them also it is not so good to make investment in Tax Free Bonds because the net return after tax will be much higher than the yield through these Bonds. Finally persons having income in excess of Rs. 5,00,000 for them it is recommended to invest in these Bonds because the net yield considering income-tax will be higher for them in Tax Free Bonds vs. the Bank Fixed deposit.

❑❑❑

3

Investment in Real Estate, Careful things to note now

Well, one may buy and sell a property at any mutually agreed price but the fact is that when you go to register the said property in the office of the Sub-Registrar you would find that the dealing clerk who is supposed to register you property deal would compare the sale consideration as mentioned in the sale deed with the fair market value of the property as per the rate fixed by the Sub-Registrar. The rate so fixed by the Sub-Registrar's office is known as "Circle Rate". Now if the sale consideration as mentioned in the sale deed is lower than the Circle Rate then the Stamp Duty would be calculated as per the value prescribed for Circle Rate. For example, if Anurag is purchasing a place of land in Gurgaon for Rs. 20 lakhs but the Circle Rate value of the said land as per the rate chart of the Sub-Registrar is Rs. 26 lakhs. Now in this illustration although the deal between the buyer and the seller will be for Rs. 20 lakhs but the payment of Stamp Duty by the buyer would be on Rs. 26 lakhs.

Having understood the meaning of "Circle Rate", it is now time to understand the impact of Income-tax on the sale transactions of real estate. A little unknown section 50C of the Income-tax Act, 1961 clearly mentions that the liability on Capital Gains would arise on the value of the property as fixed by the state valuation authority which generally is the Sub-Registrar. Thus, Capital Gains Tax would be calculated on the value of the property as fixed by the Stamp Valuation Authority specially when such value is higher than the declared value of the property as appearing in the sale deed. For example, in the above illustration if the property sold for Rs. 20 lakhs has Circle Rate of Rs. 26 lakhs then for the purposes of computation of capital gains the sale price of the property would be taken to be Rs. 26 lakhs. In the same illustration if the purchase price of the property is Rs. 15 lakhs, tehn as per the provisions enumerated in section 50C the quantum of Capital Gain would be Rs. 11 lakhs being the Circle Price of Rs. 26 lakhs less the cost of the property. Thus, we find that because of section 50C Anurag is required to pay capital gains on the higher amount. Whether you like it or not, but the fact remains that in view of this special provision existing in section 50C of the income-tax Act 1961 the correct system of computing the capital gains would be to take the sale consideration as the amount mentioned in the sale deed or the value as per the circle rate, whichever is higher. Do pay your taxes on account of capital gains by taking into consideration the fair value as fixed by the Stamp Valuation Authority.

Where an individual or a Hindu Undivided Family receives any immovable property after 1.10.2009 without consideration from non relatives of a value exceeding the sum of Rs. 50,000 then the stamp duty value of such property would be added as Income from Other Sources as per the provisions contained in section 56 of Income-tax Act, 1961. Now a days even for the seller whether a businessman or an investor such additions would be made to the total income. Hence real estate investments should be carefully made keeping in mind the Circle Rate.

From 1.6.2015 if the buyer or seller enters into cash transaction of real estate by cash in excess of Rs. 20,000 then penalty would be levied in terms of sections 269SS/269T of the Income-tax Act, 1961. The investors should remember now never to have real estate transaction by cash or bearer cheque and that to avoid any problems at a later date always buy or sell all your real estate by entering into transactions by account payee cheques or bank drafts or by RTGS.

❑❑❑

4

Investment in Residential House Property – How to claim deduction from employer

In the recent past, salaried employees have shown keen interest in taking advantage of the tax provisions by making investment in the residential house property. It is very well known fact that salaried employee like any other tax payer were to construct a residential house property or were to buy a residential house property by taking loan then he would enjoy a special deduction in respect of interest on loan to the maximum extent of Rs. 2,00,000 per annum. Now comes the next very important question and i.e. how to claim deduction from the employer itself in respect of the interest which is paid or which is payable in respect of self-occupied residential property. Well, under the provisions of the Income-tax Act, 1961, it is possible for the employer to grant deduction to the employee in respect of the loss by way of interest in respect of the property so purchased by the employee. The biggest advantage of this deduction is that the Interest so payable in respect of the housing loan is deducted by the employer from the salary income of the employee. Thus, without going to the tax department the employee is able enjoy tax concession or tax benefit in respect of interest payment on the housing loan direct from the hands of the employer.

Well to enjoy this big bonus benefit of gaining the deduction right from the employer in respect of interest on the housing loan there are certain obligations which are cast on the employee. The employee should very carefully understand these obligations and comply with the formalities as are required by the law and thereafter submit necessary papers and details concerning the interest on loan to the employer. It may please be noted that if these formalities are not complied with and if the detail pertaining to the interest on housing loan etc. is not provided to the employer in that event the employer will not be under any obligation to grant deduction in respect of the interest on the housing loan for self-occupied property. It is also worthwhile to note that if due to non-submission of the papers from the end of the employee if the employer does not grant deduction in respect of the interest on the housing loan to the employee than the employer will be deducting the income-tax on the gross total salary income without giving any benefit or deduction or rebate in respect of the interest on the housing loan. If the employer does not grant necessary deduction in respect of the housing loan due to non-submission of the papers or details etc. by the employee to the employer, in that event, the employee will have no option except to proceed for claiming the deduction by filing the Income-tax Return. Although it is possible to claim the deduction even at the time of filing the return but that would be not a good investment decision because the tax had already been deducted at source on the salary income by the employer without the deduction being granted in respect of the housing loan interest.

Now, let us see very briefly as to how to go about so as to claim a deduction right from the employer in respect of interest on the housing loan on account of capital borrowed for residential property. To claim this deduction of interest in the first phase please do remember that you take loan for housing after 1 April, 1999, and this loan can be from any person or organization and that the loan should be for constructing or acquiring the residential house and the construction or acquisition of such residential unit out of such loan amount has to be completed within three years from the end of the financial year in which the capital is borrowed. Further please do remember that the most important point to claim the deduction in respect of the interest on housing loan upto Rs. 2,00,000 would be that the employee has to furnish before the DDO a certificate from the person to whom any interest is payable on the borrowed capital specifying the amount of interest payable. In case a new loan is taken to repay the earlier loan, then the certificate should also show the details of principal and interest of the loan so repaid.

❑❑❑

5

Tax Benefits to Married Couples through Investment Planning

After marriage the married couple may face lot of family related problems in their day to day life but the fact remains that one special benefit which can be enjoyed by the married couple is the benefit relating to income-tax saving. Don't laugh it of, but the fact remains that once you get married, you are able to save lot of income tax by tax saving vistas within the framework of the Income-tax Law and suddenly you start realizing that saving income-tax after marriage is also one of the important milestones achieved by you in your life as a result of your marriage. In this article an attempt has been made to crystallize the various tax benefits which can be enjoyed by married couples within the framework of the Income-tax Law.

The first most important benefit which the married couple can enjoy is with reference to starting of a separate independent income-tax file of the spouse. It is a well known fact that every individual is not required to pay income-tax on yearly income up to Rs. 2,50,000. This happens to be the basic exemption limit up to which there is no liability on the tax payer to make payment of income-tax. Before marriage the advantage of basic income-tax exemption limit was available only to you. But now once you have got married, even your wife will be treated as a separate income-tax assessee under the provisions of the Income-tax Law. Hence, the biggest tax benefit available to an individual as a result of marriage is with reference to setting up a separate independent income-tax file of his wife. Just like a male individual the wife will also be able to enjoy income-tax benefit on income-tax exemption on income up to Rs. 2,50,000. Similarly, the tax benefit as contained in section 80C of the Income-tax Act, 1961 will be separately available to the husband as well as to the wife. Hence, on investment in Public Provident Fund or investment in taking out a Life Insurance Policy the married couple now can save income-tax by availing the tax deduction under section 80C to the tune of Rs. 1,50,000 for the husband and similar deduction also available up to Rs. 1 lakh to the wife. Thus, two separate PPF i.e. Public Provident Fund accounts can be opened by the couple consequent to marriage. Likewise, the couple independently will be able to enjoy the tax deduction in respect of section 80D of the Income-tax Act, 1961 in respect of Mediclaim policies taken by them. Likewise, if the couple finds that they are not investor right now in the stock market, then both of them can independently claim deduction under section 80CCG of the Income-tax Act, 1961 in respect of investment in the stock market. It may recalled here that the maximum deduction which can be claimed in terms of the above section is on investment of Rs. 50,000 and the deduction permissible is at the rate of 50 per cent. Hence it is crystal clear that good amount of tax saving is possible if the married couple were to think of having a separate independent Income-tax file for each of them. Another very big tax benefit available to the married couple is with reference to purchase of a residential house by taking loan. Under the provisions of the Income-tax Law if a person purchases a residential house by taking a loan and makes payment of the interest on loan, in that situation he is entitled to claim a deduction under the Income-tax Law as per section 24 of the Income-tax Act on interest payment for such residential house property. The maximum amount of interest which can be allowed as a deduction is Rs.2,00,000 per annum. Now after the marriage it is worthwhile to think of buying a house property in the name of the husband as well as in the name of the wife so that both of them independently can get the benefit of tax deduction in terms of section 24 on account of interest paid on residential house property. It may also be noted that when the husband and wife both of them they are separate tax payers, they may even think of buying one single property jointly and thereby claim deduction on account on interest on loan to the extent of Rs. 2,00,000 individually. Thus, it implies that even if one single house property is purchased jointly by husband as well as the wife and substantial amount of interest on housing loan is paid in respect of the said residential property, then the husband as well as the wife both of them would be entitled to tax deduction of Rs. 2,00,000 individually. In this manner the advantage to the married couple is that they can claim a total deduction of Rs. 3 lakhs towards interest on housing loan.

In the years to come lakhs of rupees can be saved by the married couple under the provisions of the Income-tax Law if after marriage they were to think of starting a separate tax unit in the name of a Hindu Undivided Family. The new entity by the name of Hindu Undivided Family can come into existence only after the marriage. Hence, the married couple has an added advantage of starting a separate independent Income-tax file of his Hindu Undivided Family.

However, whenever we talk of tax benefits to the married couple, please note that the young couple in particular should try to avoid making a gift to the spouse because if the gift is made by the husband to the wife or reversely if the gift is made by wife to the husband, in that situation the provisions of section 64 of the Income-tax Law would be attracted and the income would be clubbed consequent to such gift. Hence, always avoid making a gift to your spouse. Even after knowing the clubbing provisions you would like to make a gift to your dear wife then let her invest the money in tax free investment options like investing in PPF account or in Tax Free Bonds.

I would like to suggest to my reads a very interesting "Family Peace Formula" applicable for married couples. By reading the above mentioned tax benefits which are available to the married couples I am sure most of the married couples would have now thought of starting a separate income-tax file of the wife. Here I will like to share with the readers a wonderful great family peace formula innovated by me. The family peace formula is that take advantage of the provisions of the income-tax Law and start a separate independent income-tax file of your wife. Later on in due course all expenses relating to day to day running of the house i.e. all your household expenses as also children education fee, your holidays, your medical expenses i.e., for all such type of expenses let the husband make the payment of the expenses from his account. Hence, the simple theme is that the husband will incur all the expenses for the household drawings while from out of the funds belonging to the wife, the wife will go on spending the money only for making investments and saving in her name. I have found with my experience in last over 45 years that this "Family Peace Formula" would be of great advantage to the married couples and it will be also a practical bond for ever lasting marriage in the years to come. Now from practical angle this type of innovative idea will ultimately mean more safety, security of your wife and will also do away with your worries and tensions about safety, security of the wife because each year the overall net saving in the family is more in the name of your wife in comparison with the net saving in the name of the husband. I am sure the readers would find this theme interesting and the real impact of higher happiness will be seen by the married couples as and when the time passes by.

❑❑❑

6

Zero Income-tax Payment by an Individual

It would be a very wonderful idea of not paying Income-tax at all by an Individual tax payer even if he has big amount of income in his name. For this purpose tax and investment planning have to be adopted.

The first important point to be take care of is to understand the Income-tax Rates as are applicable for the financial year 2015-16 relevant to the assessment Year 2016-17.

The rates of income tax for computation of "Advance Tax" etc. during the F.Y. 2015-16 relevant to the A.Y. 2016-17 for resident individuals, HUFs, AoPs. Body of individuals and artificial juridical persons are as under:-

Up to Rs. 2,50,000	Nil
From Rs. 2,50,001 to Rs. 5,00,000	10%
From Rs. 5,00,001 to Rs. 10,00,000	20%
Above Rs. 10,00,000	30%

In the case of every resident Individual, who is of the age of 60 years or more but less than 80 years at any time during the previous year, the I.T. rates are:-

Up to Rs. 3,00,000	Nil
From Rs. 3,00,001 to Rs. 5,00,000	10%
From Rs. 5,00,001 to Rs. 10,00,000	20%
Above Rs. 10,00,000	30%

In the case of every resident individual who is of the age of 80 years or more at any time during the previous year, the rates of income tax are:-

Up to Rs. 5,00,000	Nil
Rs. 5,00,001 to Rs. 10,00,000	20%
Above Rs. 10,00,000	30%

The income tax calculated at the above rates shall be increased by a surcharge at the rate of 12% of such I.T. for a person having a total income exceeding Rs. 1,00,00,000. Education cess on I.T. and Secondary & Higher Education Cess on I.T. would continue @ 2% and 1% in all cases.

Now it is time to take advantage of various exemptions & deductions as are available to the individual tax payer. These deductions and exemptions may vary slightly for salaried employees and non salaried tax payers.

The Finance Minister in his Budget Speech for 2015-2016 has clearly stated that the individual tax payer will get tax benefit of Rs. 4,44,200 as per following details for the financial year 2015-16:

• Deduction under section 80C	Rs. 1,50,000
• Deduction under section 80CCD	Rs. 50,000
• Deduction on account of interest on house property loan (self	Rs. 2,00,000
• Occupied property)	
• Deduction under section 80D on health insurance premium	Rs. 25,000
• Exemption of transport allowance	Rs. 19,200
Total	**Rs. 4,44,200**

The following example will give a quick insight into various tax benefits which can be enjoyed by a tax payer.

Let us presume that a salaried employee receives a salary of Rs. 7,44,200 inclusive of Transport Allowance of Rs. 19,200. Besides, his income is from savings Bank account amounting to Rs. 10,000 and Dividend income of Rs. 10,000. He also has a housing loan interest payment of Rs. 2,00,000. He invests & incurs various expenses which enjoy tax deduction. His tax on his total income would now be NIL as per the following computation of total income for the financial year 2015-16 relevant to A.Y. 2016-17.

	Rs.
Salary Income	7,44,200
Interest from Savings Bank	10,000
Dividend from companies	10,000
Gross Total Income	**7,64,200**
Less	
1. Deduction from Transport Allowance as the same is now exempted @ Rs. 1,600 per month	19,200
2. Exempted Income being Dividend Income	10,000
3. Savings Bank account interest being exempted upto Rs. 10,000	10,000
4. Interest for housing loan	2,00,000
5. Deduction under section 80C for Insurance Premium, PF, PPF etc. etc.	1,50,000
6. New extra deduction under section 80CCD(1B) for investment in pension scheme	50,000
7. Deduction for Mediclaim Policy for self & family	25,000
8. Deduction for Mediclaim Policy for Parents who are senior citizens	30,000
Net Taxable Income	**2,70,000**
Tax Payable	**2,000**
Less: Rebate under Section 87A	**2,000**
Balance Tax payable	**NIL**

The above is the sample of important tax benefit which are taken into planning your taxable income of the financial year 2015-16 specially of a salaried employee.

For best planning try to have tax planning for every member of the family so that maximum tax planning can be achieved in a legal manner. Under the same facts if they pertain to a person in business he would not pay tax upto Rs. 7,45,000. Slightly lower would be the zero tax liability on HUF. The senior citizen and the very senior citizens would be able to have higher tax free zero tax payable plans due to higher tax exemption for them. Hence, plan now to have a tax free income in the above manner for every family member so that your tax liability becomes zero for the financial year 2015-16 relevant to the A.Y. 2016-17 in tune with the new provisions introduced by the Union Budget 2015-16. Invest your money in such a manner that you achieve the maximum from your investments keeping in mind the safety of your investments.

❑❑❑

7

First Investment Mantra: Decide in Whose Name to Make the Investment

The first Investment Mantra is that whenever you want to make any investment, then it is time for you now to first of all decide in whose name to make the investment. Depending upon the age group of different family members as also the present income of different family members and finally the expected income on the new investment are the pointers which should be screened before making any investment either in immovable asset or movable assets. Your investment would be best if the above mentioned parameters are taken into consideration before making any investment. Even if the amount to be invested happens to be small amount, it definitely makes the sense to plan your investment strategy well in advance and decide right now the name of the family member in whose name to invest. It is worthwhile to prepare a small chart of the impact of the income-tax, the wealth tax etc. if a particular investment is made in the name of a particular family member. Hence, before jumping to make your investment for each family member prepare a chart and see the economics of net yield specially depending on the other income of that family member. If the investment is going to take place in such instrument the income of which is completely tax free, then it would make no difference, whether the investment is made in the name of the senior most family member or in the name of the junior most family member.

❑❑❑

8

Investment Mantra for Jewellery Purchase

Jewellery! Do you love jewellery? Well, this question if is posed to any woman, the answer would be obviously, a big yes, yes. From the point of view of investment strategy before contemplating to purchase jewellery, it is worthwhile to find out the best investment mantra with regard to investment in jewellery. But before taking a lead into the final answer, the final decision of making purchase of jewellery, one should ask oneself a simple little question as to what is the purpose and object of purchasing the jewellery. Whenever jewellery is purchased, normally we do not think about the purpose of the jewellery and just make the investment. Generally speaking, the purpose of the jewellery may be for use by your family member or another purpose of the jewellery could be to buy the jewellery for giving away in marriage of your dear daughter or buying the jewellery for being given to your daughter-in-law after the marriage of your son and finally the purpose of buying jewellery is just to make profit by selling it at a later point of time. Hence, before making your investment in jewellery you must always ponder in advance as to what really your objective for making investment in jewellery. In case the purpose of making investment of the jewellery is for use by your wife or any other family member, then your investment strategy should be to buy the jewellery in the name of that family member who has got heavy wealth and heavy income whereby the tax liability is also very heavy.

If a decision is taken to invest in jewellery in the name of a family member having higher income, then obviously the biggest advantage is that income producing wealth is invested in purchasing jewellery thereby not yielding any income on the investment and this action plan would be good to make some income-tax saving in the family. For example if Rs.3 lakhs is to spent on your investment in buying new jewellery, it would be worthwhile to buy this jewellery from the funds of the husband specially, if he has got heavy salary income or business income or any other income. The net impact of buying jewellery out of the funds of the husband would mean that the income producing bank balance gets converted into jewellery which happens to be an investment yielding no income thereby for income-tax purposes the income gets reduced. However, in terms of clubbing of income provisions, the jewellery if purchased by the husband and given to the wife, then for wealth tax purpose it would be treated as the wealth of the husband only. This, however, would not create much impact on taxation front. If in this situation the jewellery was purchased in the name of the wife and her available surplus funds are not too big, then it would mean that the money thus invested by the wife in purchase of the jewellery would go to reduce the total income of the wife. Thus, it is implied that generally speaking the investment mantra is that invest in jewellery out of the funds of that family member who has got high income and high tax liability so that investment in jewellery goes to reduce the income of that high tax payer family member.

❑❑❑

9

Investment in Real Estate for Fixed Rental Income

If you are thinking of making investment in Real Estate so as to receive a fixed rental income by letting out property, then such property can be purchased in the name of any member of the family including a family member with heavy tax liability and heavy income. This is because of the fact that in respect of the rental income derived by you, you are eligible to enjoy a tax deduction of 30 per cent from the rental income which indirectly means that the maximum income-tax liability in respect of your rental income would be 21 per cent only. It is this standard deduction from rental income available in the Income-tax Law that would inspire every investor to make investment in real estate for receiving a fixed rental income. Do remember that irrespective of your quantum of rental income the maximum income-tax payable after availing the standard deduction from rental income would be just 21 per cent only. Hence, it is better for persons with high income to go in for investment in real estate for fixed rental income. Another very important point to remember with reference to buying a property for renting out is that buy such property with loan as the entire amount of interest on such loan would be allowed deduction.

❑❑❑

10

Investment in Unit Linked Insurance Policy

For most tax payers it is not worth to invest in Unit Linked Insurance Policy. Generally people invest in insurance policies with unit plan so as to achieve the benefits of insurance on the one hand and also to enjoy the benefit of investment in the Mutual Fund. However, the Investment Mantra is that if you want to achieve the benefit of insurance, better take a separate insurance policy. Likewise, if you want to achieve the gains and fruits of Mutual Fund, then better go in for separate investment in Mutual Funds only and as far as possible don't make investment in Unit Linked Insurance Plan. In the short term definitely the Unit Linked Insurance Policies (ULIPs) are not efficient investment tools. However, in the long term they may be beneficial. Hence, in most cases it would be worthwhile to make investment by taking out insurance policy and also taking out separate investment in the Mutual Fund.

You want insurance cover for your family and you also want Mutual Fund Investment. Hence you take a decision to invest in ULIP (Unit Link Insurance Plan) whereby you take out a simple Life Insurance Policy for yourself and the Insurance company makes the investment of your funds in taking out Insurance Policy thereby making the investment in Mutual Fund Units also. Well, to achieve the best results it is recommended that if you want insurance for your family, better take a specific insurance policy and similarly when you want the investment in Mutual Fund also take out very simple Mutual Fund.

11

Investment in New Pension Scheme

It is time now to start investing in New Pension Scheme. Please focus your investment strategy on the investment vistas related to the New Pension Scheme. The New Pension Scheme into operation for the last couple of years, but it has not become very popular. It is time to go for the NPS. Study the provisions in detail and try to open separate NPS account for different members in your family. For those tax payers who have high income and considerable wealth. It is recommended that the Tier II account in NPS should also be obtained. If you are completing 60 this year, you shold be more careful to immediately open the NPS account in your name. This is mainly because once you have completed 60, you cannot open a new NPS Account. But if you have already one you can continue contributing to it. Do remember that if you invest in contributing upto Rs. 50,000 in the Pension Scheme of the Central Government, then you enjoy an additional deduction over and above the deduction under section 80C and the additional deduction is as per the provisions contained in Section 80CCB(1B) of the Income-tax Act, 1961. In comparison with the yield on various Mutual Funds the yield in respect of NPS investment will be slightly higher because of cost control in the management of the fund.

For more details contact:

www.pfrda.org.in

❑❑❑

12

Invest in Government Approved Industrial Plots

Invest now in Govt. recognized and Govt. approved Industrial Plots in different parts of India. It is time now to think of starting some industrial activity. If you do not have anything in mind, even then it makes a sense to book your industrial plot and thereafter think of starting industrial activity thereon. The best time to invest in the industrial plot is at the time when the Government just opens the scheme in respect of the new Industrial estate developed by the Government. Later on due to some reason if you are unable to set up your industry, then also it makes the sense to reap the rich fruits on your investment in the said industrial plot.

As per the Finance Act, 2015 very high Depreciation as also Investment Allowance would be available in industrial belts of Andhra Pradesh, Telangana, Bihar and West Bengal. Hence, investment in Industrial Plots in these areas should be preferred investment for Industrial Plots.

❑❑❑

13

Invest in a Vacant Plot of Land for Your Minor Child

The best investment which you can think of specially if you have got a minor son or a daughter is to make the investment in a vacant plot of land or in agricultural land. When your aim is to multiply the investment made in the name of your minor children, then do not make the investment in a residential flat etc. in the name of the minor child but the best investment to bring for you rich fruits to you for your investment in the name of your minor child is to invest in a vacant plot of land. If you have got more than one child, then best would be to invest in vacant plot in the name of each child. Hence, if you can afford better make investment in the name of each of your child for one vacant plot of land so that by the time the child becomes major, the value of the plot will appreciate so much so as to take care of his higher education, his marriage and settling him in business. The provisions relating to clubbing of income of the minor child under the Income-tax Law will also not present any problem specially when the plot is purchased by the father or the mother in the name of the minor children because from the vacant plot of land no income is going to come. Hence, there will be no impact of clubbing of income of the minor children. Smart Cities are being developed, hence investment in these new smart cities would be good investment.

❑❑❑

14

Formula to Double Your Retirement Benefits

When you retire, you are likely to receive approximately 25 to 50 lakhs of rupees all inclusive comprising of Gratuity Amount, Provident Fund Amount and other retirement benefits. It is true that such big amount will be received by you generally once in life time. For most investors the retirement amount so received would be biggest amount which they have seen in their life. If you are interested to have the benefit of second retirement money i.e. if you want to receive double the amount of your retirement, then the Investment Mantra is that while you are in active service, invest in one residential plot of land. Forget this land and just encash it at the time when you are going to retire and receive your retirement benefits. This one single piece of land which you have purchased couple of years ago if sold at the time of your retirement, will bring in substantial money to be made available for your future investment and will actually be like a second retirement benefit. Hence, to reap the fruits of receiving double retirement benefit, do plan now and invest in one piece of land so that the big money which you get at the time of your retirement, you can fulfill all your family commitments, old age commitments and other connected matters.

❑❑❑

15

Divide and Rule Your Investments

One of the very wonderful Investment Mantra is that always prepare a Financial Planner for every investment which you are looking for in the family. Hence, every investor should divide broadly his entire investments under the following groups and then alone decide the percentage of investment as per the family situation and requirement:

1. Zero Risk Investment
2. Investment in the Equity Market
3. Investment in Mutual Fund
4. Investment in Real Estate
5. Investment in Insurance Policy
6. Risky Investment Options
7. Jewellery and other Investments

One should divide the entire gamut of his investment portfolio in the above manner and then you are able to reap the best fruits on all your investments. Also do remember never to invest your entire money in one single basket of investment. The old saying that 'never keep all eggs in one basket' even holds good today. Out of the seven boxes of investment which are available with you, how much to invest in a particular set of investment will depend upon various matters including the age group etc. It is recommended that for persons who are 70 plus, their 50 per cent of the total funds must be invested in non-risky investment instruments or Zero Risk Investment Instruments including Bank/ Fixed Deposit, Debt Mutual Funds, Bonds of Reserve Bank of India. Similarly, another 20 per cent of their funds should be invested in Equity Related Mutual Funds and 15 per cent in Real Estate while 10 per cent to be invested in jewellery etc. and just 5 per cent may be invested in lucrative risky investment proposals. Similarly, if a person is in the age group of 50 years plus, he can opt to invest just 30 per cent of his total available surplus in Non-Risky Zero Risk Investment Proposals and Bank FDR etc. while he may go for investment up to 10 per cent of his fund in the Equity Mutual Funds. This age group of persons may invest 20 per cent in Real Estate Sector, 10 per cent in Insurance Sector and 20 per cent investment in Risky Investment proposals. In the case of very young investor like the age group of 20/30 years he can safely invest at least up to 40% of his total funds in the Equity market or Equity Related Mutual Funds as also 10 per cent in Real Estate, 20 per cent in Insurance and 30 per cent he can go in for Risky Investment Proposals. The above mentioned guide of Investment strategy may vary depending upon the facts and circumstances of the investor, his family size, his money requirement etc. However, one should always prepare a Financial Planner and only then make the Investment Strategy befitting to the requirement.

❑❑❑

16

Investment in Gold Mutual Funds

Ladies will not stop to buy jewellery. That is a fact. But first analyse that your investment in jewellery will result into lower yield of your investment returns sepcially if you are planning to sell the jewellery at a later stage and buy some other jewellery. For other persons who are interested to buy jewellery or who are interested to make investment in jewellery, then such persons should not buy jewellery but should invest only in Gold Bars, Silvr Bars and lose diamonds. Do remember that when your strategy is to sell jewellery and again invest in some new jewellery, it would make sense not to buy jewellery because when you sell it, you will not be able to get a better yield. If you remake the jewellery, then making charges are payable and substantial loss is also there. Hence, the best way is to invest in Gold Bars and not just jewellery more particularly if you want to sell the same other sometime. You can also think of investing in Gold Mutual Funds and in NIFTY Bees, so that gold is not kept in physical form. From the point of investment gold is not recommended.

❑❑❑

17

Single Premium Insurance Policy

Specially when you are not sure about the cash flow position at different intervals in your life, then it surely makes a sense for you to go in for making investment in a single premium insurance policy whereby you take out an insurance policy and make payment for the insurance premium but that happens to be just one time payment only. It is easy for you to keep track of the onetime payment and you find no hassles and no tensions in the years to follow and you have not to remember to make the insurance premium every year or every quarter. Question now arises as to whether the premium paid under single insurance policy would be tax deductible and whether the amount received on maturity would be tax exempt? Well if we screen carefully the provisions as are enumerated in section 80C of the Income-tax Act, 1961, we find that under the whole Income-tax Act there is no prohibition with regard to payment in respect of single insurance premium policy. However, what is to be taken care of is that to ensure that the sum assured happens to be more than five times the value of the premium which has been paid. Once you take small little care of this aspect, then you have no hassles and tensions in taking out a single premium insurance policy and claiming a tax deduction on the same. Likewise, when the maturity proceeds are received even in respect of single premium policies, the amount so received would be exempt from income-tax as per section 10(10D) of the Income-tax Act, 1961. But this is possible only when you find that the premium for the single premium policy should never be in excess of 10 per cent of the sum assured. Hence the investment mantra is to take out single premium policy with longer maturity value and claim thereon the benefit of income-tax deduction and also the benefit of tax exemption. Single premium policy has great advantage specially in the case of management of good inflow of the funds which you were not expecting. For example if you are going to get some big bonus amount but you are also not sure to receive such big amount on regular basis in the years to follow, then surely it makes a sense to take out a single premium policy out of the funds which you have received on account of bonus or arrear salary etc.

❑❑❑

18

Invest in Residential House with Loan

Making investment in a residential house property by taking loan is definitely one of the wonderful investment mantra which makes you buy your house on the one hand while on the other hand taking a loan for the house property brings for you a tax deduction in the form of deduction for interest payment to the tune of Rs.2 lakh per annum in terms of section 24 of the Income-tax Act, 1961. However, if you wish to get a deduction in respect of interest on housing loan, not upto Rs.2 lakh but upto Rs. 4 lakhs per annum, then yes there is a legal way whereby your proper investment in house property by taking loan can make you achieve a tax deduction in your family to the tune of Rs.4 lakhs per annum in respect of the interest which you have paid. Well, the simple legal formula to enjoy a tax deduction on your investment in residential house property by taking loan is to buy the property jointly in the name of husband as well as the wife so that each person takes a loan on his or her share in the property and thereby each of them will be eligible to claim a tax deduction of Rs. 2 lakhs per annum in respect of the interest on loan. Please do remember that each co-owner of the property is entitled to separate deduction in respect of interest payment for house property purchased on loan to the tune of Rs. 2 lakhs. Please also note that the loan for residential house property can be taken from the bank, any other financial institution, the employer or friend or relative or any other person. Under the tax law there is no restriction on claiming tax deduction in respect of interest on loan for residential property paid to any person at any rate of interest.

❑❑❑

19

Investment in Minor Child Name and Still No Clubbing of Income

Plan your investment in such a manner that even if you make investment in the name of your minor child, still the income from such investment is not added with your income. If you can achieve this in real life, then surely you will be able to cut down your burden of taxes and your investment will bring better yield for you and your family. It is well known fact that the income of the minor child is clubbed or added with the income of the father or mother. This would be the situation even when the gift etc. in the name of the minor child is received not from the parents but from other relatives. Thus, it is crystal clear that even if you receive gift from a relative, even then the income of the minor child will be added to the income of the parents. For example let us say Master Anurag receives a gift of Rs.1 lakh from his father Bikash. Likewise, Anurag also receives a gift of Rs.1 lakh from his Nani Sushila. Now the sum of Rs.2 lakhs received by way of gift is invested in the name of Anurag in the bank Fixed Deposit where the bank interest is 9 per cent per annum. The total yearly interest comes to Rs.18,000 in respect of the gift from the father and also gift from other relative. The entire amount of interest in respect of both the gifts would however be added to the income of Bikash. Now it is presumed that Bikash is having taxable income much more than Rs.10 lakhs per annum in which case income-tax payable on the sum of Rs.18,000 being interest income on bank Fixed Deposit in the name of his minor child Anurag will bring extra income tax liability on the said Rs.18,000 at the rate of 30 per cent which comes to Rs.5,400. This amount of Rs.5,400 would be the income-tax liability payable in respect of the interest belonging to minor son Anurag which has been added to the income of his father Bikash. Now the best investment mantra for persons like Bikash and all other persons who have a minor child in the family is to set up a 100 per cent Specific Beneficiary Trust in the name of the minor child and make the gift in the name of the said Trust. Now based on the very famous and important decision of the Supreme Court of India in the case of M.R. Doshi the income of this 100 per cent Specific Beneficiary Trust of the minor child will not be added to the income of father or mother of the minor child specially when the Trust Deed provides that so long as the child is a minor, no money will be spent on the minor child. Hence, the important investment mantra is that all persons having a minor child in the family who would like to plan the investment for their minor child should create a specific Trust for the minor beneficiary keeping in view the decided principles of the law as per the above mentioned Supreme Court of India's decision in the case of M.R. Doshi and thus avoid the clubbing of income of the minor child to their income. Substantial tax saving is possible so also separate funds for the minor also possible if you resort to creating a Specific Beneficiary Trust of your minor child.

❑❑❑

20

Investment in Real Estate by Non Resident Indians

If you are a Non-resident Indian and you are interested to make investment in Real Estate in India, then before making this investment in Real Estate, kindly have a look at FEMA provisions which are contained in Foreign Exchange Management (Acquisition and Transfer of immovable property in India) Regulations, 2000. This is modified by the Reserve Bank of India from time to time. Hence, you can visit the website of FEMA to have the latest update on the subject. However, please note that all Non-resident Indians can hold, own or transfer immovable property in India without any specific condition. In terms of the above mentioned regulation and specially as contained in Regulation No. 3 of the said regulation mentioned above, an Indian citizen resident outside India is permitted to acquire any immovable property in India other than agricultural land, plantation property or a farm house. Hence, the Non-resident Indians should not purchase agricultural land as also farm house in India. However, the Non-resident Indians can transfer any property in India to any person resident in India. Likewise application for immovable property for permitted activity is also possible for the Non-resident Indians. The repatriation of the sale proceeds is also easy in respect of the property purchased in India. The Non-resident Indians can also inherit immovable properties and also can receive immovable property by way of gift. Thus, the investment in Real Estate is possible without any hassles for a Non-resident Indian either by way of purchase or by way of receiving the property as a gift or even by way of receiving the property by way of inheritance from friends and relatives. The formalities and procedures for repatriation of the sale proceeds of immovable property are also simple and easy which makes investment in immovable property a very lucrative investment for all those Non-resident Indians who are settled in abroad.

❑❑❑

21

Investment in Cheap Agricultural Land

In some States of India it is not possible for the investors to make an investment in the agricultural land. One may be surprised as to how this is possible specially when I have bag full of money and I go in the market and I want to buy the agricultural land but unable to buy it. What stops me! Well, the law still exists in some States of India where you cannot freely go and make purchase of agricultural land in your name. In these States there is a law that only the agriculturists can purchase agricultural land. And, you are not an agriculturist. So you find that it is virtually impossible to buy a piece of agricultural land in that State. In such situation the practical answer for you which will enable you to purchase the agricultural land in that State is that now go and buy a small piece of agricultural land in some other States where there are no rules or regulations or restrictions for purchasing agricultural land. Once you have purchased agricultural land in some other States of India where there are no hassles and no tension and you become the proud owner of a small piece of agricultural land in that State. Now come to the State in which you want to buy the agricultural land. Now you can easily buy your dream agricultural land in this State in spite of not being an agriculturist of that State but as you are agriculturist of some other State of India holding valid documents and papers, then it is easy for you to make the purchase of agricultural land in the other State where there is a restriction for sale of land to non-agriculturist. In the end, you become agriculturist of one state and buy land in the other state. Let's buying cheap agricultural land be your one of the most important investment mantra of your life. Yes, believe me it is definitely going to be a wonderful experience to buy cheapest available agricultural land in any part of India. I have seen in my last four decades that the maximum growth of investment has been best achieved for all those investors who got agricultural land at cheapest available price. Please do remember that not merely in your town or in your State or in India but in the whole of the world the space is limited. Money power is coming in the hands of all those persons who till yesterday had no money power. Same has been the experience for you. I believe now when people will have more money to buy and to invest, then surely the price of your Real Estate in the form of cheapest available agricultural land will rise at phenomenal level. Hence, it is time now for you to think of making your investment entry in the field of buying cheap agricultural land. I am always in favour of making investment in cheap agricultural land and never in costly agricultural land.

❑❑❑

22

No Divorce to your Share Purchase

No divorce to your share purchase. This should be your guiding principle if you want to make more money in the investment which you make in your shares specially if you purchase Government company shares, it is better to get married to these shares for a longer duration. Hence, in real life as you avoid the situation of divorce, so also would be situation of your marriage to good shares of companies. It is worthwhile not to ever think of having a divorce with such investment. Specially if you look from the point of view of your old age investment strategy, it definitely makes a sense to preserve the investment made by you in the form of shares of Government Companies and blue chip companies in particular. Hence, invest today as little as you would like to, no problem at all but still stay married to such shares for a pretty very long time. This thinking of yours will definitely make your golden years more cheerful with no hassles and no tension regarding the money and the expenses during your retirement age.

Just like we celebrate our silver jubilee of marriage anniversary on the same pattern and theme if you decide to celebrate the silver jubilee of some of the shares then surely your investment will bring rich dividends for you.

❑❑❑

23

Investment in Equity Linked Savings

Invest in the best Equity Linked Savings Scheme (ELSS) so as to enjoy tax free income on the one hand and also to enjoy a deduction in respect of the investment which you have made today. Do remember that you can make the investment in Equity Linked Savings Scheme and enjoy a deduction under section 80C of the Income-tax Act, 1961 within the overall limit of Rs.1.5 lakh. The question now arises is which ELSS Scheme to invest in. This is the most important point on which you have to get the answer. Finding answer is not that simple and easy. But here is the practical formula that will make you reap your best returns on the investment which you make in Equity Linked Savings Scheme. Well here is the formula - check list of the top funds performing best in last two years in respect of the Equity Linked Savings Schemes offered by them. Now out of this list of ten funds just choose any four top funds and divide your entire investible amount of Equity Linked Savings Scheme Investment in the four funds, now invest and just relax. My experience is that your yield would be very good one if you make investment in four or five top schemes of ELSS out of the top ten fund which have performed well in last one year. Going in for just one single Mutual Fund whose scheme of ELSS has faired the best one may not bring the desired results for you in the coming years. Hence, do plan your strategy in such a manner that you are able to get the best yield on your investment in Equity Linked Savings Scheme. So just remember the simple formula for your investment in Equity Linked Savings Schemes is divide and rule. Yes do divide your entire available surplus to be invested in 3/4 instruments of ELSS issued by different companies and then as you see for yourself one of the wonderful appreciations of the investment you have made.

In the last few years we have seen that the investment in ELSS has not given the desired results to the investors. But I feel that in years to follow remaining attached with ELSS investment would have good return on their investment.

❑❑❑

24

Health Insurance Policy

Investment in taking out a Health Insurance not just for you but for your family is equally a good tool of investment strategy. Just imagine if you would not have taken out a Health Insurance Policy and if some of the family members were to get serious illness then a big portion of the amount of your existing invested funds would be melted away because from investments the amount would go away to the hospital for making payment of hospital bills for your treatment and treatment of your family members. Hence, do take out a Health Insurance Policy and please be careful to make payment of the yearly renewal for this Health Insurance Policy in time. In most cases you will find that the Health Insurance Company issuing you the policy will take no efforts to send you reminders to renew your Health Insurance Policy. Hence, it is time for you now to take out a Health Insurance Policy and thereafter to remember making payment of yearly Health Insurance premium much ahead of the due date so that the Policy does not lapse. For Health insurance the best is to take out the policy at a young age. Also do remember that the Health Insurance Policy should be taken out not just in your name but in the name of your other family members too. Another special advantage which is available on your contribution for taking out a Health Insurance Policy is a big special tax deduction available to you in respect of the payment made by you for Health Insurance. It is within the parameters of section 80D of the Income-tax Act, 1961 that you enjoy a great big deduction for Health Insurance Premium in terms of section 80D would be available from the Financial Year 2015-16 upto Rs. 25,000. Likewise for Senior Citizens the limit for deduction will be up to Rs.30,000. Likewise the deduction available to individuals in respect of Health Insurance Premium for senior citizens parents would be eligible to tax deduction up to Rs. 30,000. For super senior citizens who are 80 plus and who do not enjoy the benefit for any tax deduction as no Mediclaim Policy is available to them. Hence, they will get deduction up to Rs. 30,000 on account of medical expenditure on the health of very senior citizens. Thus, it is time now to let your Health Insurance Policy act as a good investment protector for you so that your money is not wasted in making payments to the hospital and this is possible by taking out a Health Insurance Policy.

❑❑❑

25

Get a Free Flat for You

Do you want to get a free flat for you? Well, every investor would just say oh, just say a big yes to this question. Well taking advantage of this investment mantra is possible for you to have your ownership for flat for free. It sounds ridiculous. But the fact is that it is possible to achieve the target of receiving a free flat for you. Well, the simple principle is that you today book two flats in a upcoming residential project. To reap the best fruits of your investment try to book the flats at the initial stage itself. Now go on making payment of installments for both the flats. It will be little taxing for your pocket but yes if you want to receive a free flat for your family, then surely take this route of making payment of the installments for both the flats. Pay now the first installment. Continue paying the second, the third and other installments on due date. For timely payment discounts or concessions are available; do take advantage of the concession. Now is the time to get ready for getting your free flat, yes absolutely free with no cost at all. The theme now is once both the flats are ready, it is time for you now to sell one of the flats and retain the other flat. By doing this what happens is that by the time the flat is ready, there has been great all round appreciation of your flat and when you sell one of your flats, the amount received in comparison with the investment made by you is so big so as to make one flat available to you absolutely free of cost. Take advantage of this investment mantra and start your hunt for buying two flats under installment plan and thus have one flat free for you.

26

Invest Your Retirement Benefits in Senior Citizens Savings Scheme

You may get anything between Rs.15 lakhs to Rs.50 lakhs by way of your retirement benefits. It is time now to plan in advance the investment of this big fat money which is definitely coming to most of you once in a life time. For all those persons expecting the retirement benefits they should plan in advance as to where to use the money which flows from their retirement. Advance planning of the funds flow will help you to reap the best fruits you can think of out of your investment. The first big retirement Mantra is that say a big good bye to all your relatives and friends specially with reference to the money power. Never let the money go to the so called relatives and friends who are going to fly near you very promptly as soon as the money comes up of your retirement benefits. Before the retirement benefits get into your bank account, these relatives are there very handy to advise you all sort of things as to how to make use of the big money which you are going to get on retirement. But please say a big no to them and plan your money matters with Investment Mantra. The first step should be to invest Rs.15 lakhs in the Senior Citizens Savings Scheme. The Senior Citizens Savings Scheme Account can be opened either with a Post Office or with State Bank of India. From practical angle I would like to advise that it is better to open the account with State Bank of India with less hassles and problems. The big advantage of Senior Citizens Savings Scheme is that you get steady flow of 9.2 per cent interest per annum and that too payable quarterly and is directly credited to your bank account. Such a wonderful and safe yield cannot be seen with any other investment. Hence, do make it a point to deposit Rs.15 lakhs in the Senior Citizens Savings Account. The balance money available at your disposal should be parked in Post Office Monthly Income Plan so as to enjoy further steady yield on your investment so as to take care of your day to day household expenditure. Please do remember that the maximum amount which can be deposited in the Six Year Post Office Monthly Income Scheme is Rs.4.50 lakhs in a single account and Rs.9 lakhs in a joint account. The interest is payable at the rate of 8.4 per cent per annum. After depositing money in the Senior Citizens Savings Scheme as also in the Post Office Monthly Income Scheme now is the time to invest the balance money either in a Mutual Fund or in big Company Deposit. It is recommended that the balance funds may not be invested in Equity Linked Mutual Fund but best would be to invest in the Balance Fund of the Mutual Fund whereby the investment of the Mutual Fund is exposed to lower risk. Under the Balanced Fund invest major portion in the Debt instruments and just a small portion of money is to be invested in equity. The above investment strategy would make a best combination of your retirement funds.

❑❑❑

27

Investment Mantra for Factory Land

If you are contemplating to construct a factory of your own for starting production or if you are contemplating to erect your own office building, then the first step to do is to buy a piece of land. Here is an Investment Mantra for all those persons who are contemplating to buy land for construction either of a factory building or a office complex. Never buy factory land or office land direct in the name of your partnership concern or in the name of your Private Limited Company. Well the main reason of advising not to buy in the name of the Company or the Firm is that if you make your investment today of buying the factory land in the name of your business enterprise and thereafter construct building thereon for office or for factory, in that situation your business enterprise be it a proprietorship concern, a Private Limited Company, a Partnership or a Limited Liability Partnership, in all situations no depreciation at all will be allowed on the purchase price of the land. Hence, the Investment Mantra is that always buy this piece of land in the name of some family member so that the family member making investment in the land can lease out the land to the business enterprise and thereby the lease rent becomes the income of the individual while the pay out by the business enterprise towards the rent for the land is treated as a normal business expenditure allowed under the provisions of the Income-tax Act, 1961. This small but wonderful Investment Mantra will help you to save lakhs or crores specially if you take a decision to buy a piece of land not directly in the name of your business enterprise but in the name of some individual in the family.

❑❑❑

28

Post Office Recurring Deposit Account

Post Office Recurring Deposit Account would be very good Investment Mantra specially for housewives as also for your adult children if they are not yet earning. With as little as monthly minimum deposit of Rs.10 one can open a Post Office Recurring Deposit Account and thereafter deposit every month in multiples of Rs.5. You will be surprised to find that in this Five Year Post Office Recurring Deposit Account the sum of Rs.10 denomination will yield Rs 746.53 at maturity. Although there is no tax benefit in respect of the interest income, so also there is no tax deduction in respect of the investment made under Post Office Recurring Deposit Account but definitely it is a very good investment specially for small investors. For best results better open Post Office Recurring Deposit Account in the names of all the family members specially the adult family members. Also do not forget to show in your income-tax Return the interest income. Now the provisions of Tax Deduction At Source would be applicable on maturity.

❑❑❑

29

The Postal Investment

For all those who are looking for a small investment with no commitment of investment every month, then the Investment Mantra would be to invest in National Savings Certificate VIII Issue of the Post Office. These certificates are available in denominations of Rs.100, Rs.500, Rs.1000, Rs.5000 and Rs.10000. There is no upper limit of investment in NSC. That(makes the investment a good investment specially because you have the freedom to invest as much as you like at any point of time you like. The interest in respect of NSC Certificate is compounded half yearly at maturity. Hence, Rs.100 invested today in NSC becomes Rs. 151.62 after 5 years. For ten year investment in NSC the sum of Rs 100 becomes Rs 236.60 after 10 years. Do remember that NSC is safe and secured investment and the lock in period is 5 years and 10 years. Hence choose the NSC of your choice depending upon your financial needs. It is also recommend for all those investors who have a grown up daughter in the family with age 16 plus, it also makes the sense to make, investment in National Savings Certificate of the Post Office in the name of your minor daughter age 12 years and above so that when the maturity amount is received, at that time your daughter becomes major and the tax benefit can be achieved with no clubbing of income. Also do remember that a small little investment made by you in NSC can bring a big fortune for you to take care of your future big liability and responsibilities in the family including education of your children and also including the marriage of your daughter.

Post Office Time Deposit is also good for all such persons who may receive lump sum money either by way of arrear salary or big overtime or some big bumper money. The investment in Post Office Time Deposit is also good for all those who are going to receive some money by way of succession or inheritance so that the money can be deposited in the Post Office Time Deposit Account which can bring good deal in the form of interest bearing from 8.40 per cent for one year and going to as high as 8.50 per cent for Five Year Account. The interest is payable annually under the Post Office Time Deposit Rules, 1981 but the special feature is that such interest is calculated on quarterly basis. If you deposit money in the Post Office Time Deposit Account of five year duration, in that event you are also entitled to get a deduction in respect of the investment under section 80C within the overall limit of Rs.1.5 lakh.

❑❑❑

30

Invest in Post Office Monthly Income Scheme

If you are a retired person, a house wife, a widow or a pensioner and you are in need of monthly income to support your regular expenses, then the Investment Mantra for you is to deposit your money in the Six Year Post Office Monthly Income Scheme of the Post Office. The minimum amount with which you can open the Post Office Monthly Income Account is Rs. 1,500 while the maximum amount which can be deposited by you in the Post Office Monthly Income Scheme is Rs.4.50 lakhs in a single account. If, however, you are having a joint account with your spouse or with any other family member of yours, in that event the maximum amount which can be deposited in this Post Office Monthly Income Scheme is Rs.9 lakhs. The interest payable by the Post Office on the Monthly Income Scheme is much better than the present Fixed Deposit Interest which you get on the Bank Fixed Deposit. Presently 8.4 per cent per annum is the interest payable in respect of your investment in Post Office Monthly Income Scheme. The 8.4 per cent interest is payable monthly i.e. on deposit of Rs.12000, a sum of Rs.84 will be payable every month to you on your investment in the Post Office Monthly Income Scheme.

❑❑❑

31

Investment in Public Provident Fund Account

If you are coming in the highest income bracket of taxation and you do not have any immediate requirement for couple of years to withdraw the amount invested by you and you want complete safety, security and also tax benefit on your investment, then surely your investment in the Public Provident Fund Account would be the best Investment Mantra for such persons. Please remember that you can open a Public Provident Fund Account in the Post Office or with the State Bank of India. The minimum amount which is required for opening the PPF Account is just Rs.500 and the maximum amount which can be contributed in this PPF Account is Rs.1,50,000 in one Financial Year. The special feature is that it is not necessary to deposit the entire sum of Rs.1,50,000 at one go. Rather the investor can deposit in the PPF Account the money at regular intervals depending upon his cash flow. However, do remember that the only small problem or restriction with regard to your investment in Public Provident Fund is that you cannot deposit more than Rs.1,50,000 in one financial year in Public Provident Fund Account. It is also not permitted to open more than one PPF Account in the name of the same person. However, you can open the PPF Account in your name as also in the name of your spouse. The PPF Account now a days cannot be opened in the name of Hindu Undivided Family. While talking of the minor children, you can also take the option to open the PPF Account in the name of your minor children. Hence, if you have got one child or more than one child, you are at liberty to open different PPF Accounts in the name of your different children. However, with regard to minor children, it may be noted that the maximum amount which can be deposited in your PPF Account including the PPF Accounts in the name of your minor children is maximum sum of Rs.1,50,000 only in one Financial Year. Presently interest at the rate of 8.7 per cent is payable on your PPF Account and this interest is compounded and credited to your account at the end of each Financial Year. The minimum period for which The Public Provident Fund Account has to be maintained compulsorily is 15 years. However, after the completion of 15 years, you can extend the PPF Account by a block of five years. Another biggest advantage of your investment in Public Provident Fund Account is that the entire interest income received by you from Public Provident Fund Account is completely exempt under section 10 of the Income-tax Act, 1961. Moreover your investment in Public Provident Fund Account also brings home for you a very big special tax deduction under section 80C of the Income-tax Act, 1961. Do remember that in terms of the said section 80C you can make investment upto Rs.1.5 lakh and avail tax deduction from your income. All those who are young and who can afford to keep their money invested for a long time should definitely go in for investment in the Public Provident Fund Account so that income gets exempted and the investment also gets deduction under the tax law. For those who are in business the investment in Public Provident Fund Account is still very important because of the fact that your investment in the Public Provident Fund Account cannot be attached by any person. Hence, the investment is the safest one.

❑❑❑

32

The Collective Bargaining Power of Investors

If you want to make money in Real Estate, then you must have great faith in the collective bargaining power of the investors. Keeping in tune this principle it is time that you form a "Bulk Buyer Group" of investors comprising of your friends, relatives or acquaintances and this bulk buyers buying group should assess the investment requirement in the immovable property of their group and then approach the big builders or developers and thereafter try a big deal to get the Real Estate at a heavy discount. Please do remember that it is possible in a practical manner to achieve the success of great bargaining power by combining your friends and relatives to form your Bulk Buying Group and only then make your investment in Real Estate and then flourish. This Investment Mantra can also be replicated by members of Rotary Club, the members of Lions Club, the members of Morning Walkers Club and the members of Kitty Party. Whatever group you are attached with in social or cultural life or may be a group of friends working in the same organization, they can all combine together pulling their resources and then finally go for shopping of the Real Estate by bargaining from the developer just because of the big bargaining power they are able to have due to big buying at one go. A real life example of the money power of bulk buying group was seen recently when in Aurangabad a group of people purchased 115 Mercedes Cars and bargained with car manufacturing Company, same concept can be implemented by you for getting a good deal in the real estate sector. So now relax and try to form a group of yours or join an existing group to make most lucrative investment in real estate.

❑❑❑

33

Zero Coupon Bond – Grab it Now

Make your investment in Zero Coupon Bond to achieve wonderful return coupled with safety for you. Way back in the year 2005 Zero Coupon Bond concept was introduced for the first time in India. Later on various companies have started issuing the Zero Coupon Bonds. The National Housing Bank issued the Zero Coupon Bonds each of Rs.10000. Presently Zero Coupon Bond of which Company is available for sale has to be ascertained from the market and only then the investment has to be made. The yield is very good of the Zero Coupon Bond, the safety and security of the investment is superb, the investment horizon is ten years, and therefore, the investment in Zero Coupon Bond is going to be great specially if you are contemplating to provide safety and security for your wife and for other members in the family. It is time now to even make investment in Zero Coupon Bonds and then gift the same to your children for their safety and security. In between the maturity period one does not receive any amount or income from this Zero Coupon Bonds. Another special feature of the Zero Coupon Bonds which makes it very attractive and lucrative is that once you sell the Zero Coupon Bond, the amount which you get becomes long-term capital gains as per the provisions of the Income-tax Law. Once it is Long-term Capital Gain as per the existing concept, the capital gains will be calculated based on the theme of Cost Inflation Index. Hence, in most cases there would be no liability with regard to payment of tax on selling these Bonds. However, these Bonds would also be traded in the stock market. Hence, the liquidity would not cause much problem. A portion of your investment portfolio definitely should comprise of small little investment in Zero Coupon Bonds also.

❑❑❑

34

When to Buy Gold

Want to buy gold.. When to buy? Should I consult some astrologer of the time of buying the gold. No, not at all. Here is a wonderful astrological answer for you. This concept is going to bring some money for you for your investment in gold. Well, the simple time for buying your gold is during non-marriage season. The prices of the gold generally are very low in the non-marriage season. Hence, it makes a sense to make your investment in gold during off season of marriage and then ultimately you want to make the money, it also makes a sense to sell the gold held by you during the peak marriage season. By implementing this simple formula of buying and selling gold during off season and marriage season would mean good money to you. You want to know the topmost marriage season each year then just get hold of the Pandit in the temple and then jot down the best marriage dates in the whole of the year and thereafter start your strategy of making investment in the gold.

❑❑❑

35

Investment Mantra for Your Next Generation

The road to progress of your family can be well conceived if we have a look at one single yardstick namely appreciation of the investment made by the family. Hence, if you are concerned about the road to progress of your family and you want the younger generation in the family to make prosperity, to make great appreciation in investment, to be concerned about investment strategy and planning, then give them the under noted formula for implementation. Well, the simple formula is that let all the family members sit down at the dining table with no eatables on the table but just a piece of paper available to each one. Now you write down one figure. Say you write 15, and now you write 150 and thereafter you write 1500. Well, this is the real investment mantra for your family's prosperity and investment appreciation. To illustrate this point the theme is that supposing the head of the family gives 15 rupees to the younger generation, then he should also give a target to the said younger generation: "This 15 rupees which is given to you and you have all the powers as you like to make the investment and change the investment and withdraw from the investment and again make the investment and change the investment but continue further so that this Rs.15 should become Rs.150 in ten year." Now you give the next target to the same young generation sitting on the dining table that well your 15 rupees investment becomes Rs.150 in next 10 years. Then let it further multiply for better investment strategy from Rs.150 to Rs.1500 again in next ten years.. Now conclude your observation before the other family members that nothing more you would like to add and just give this money to the younger generation to think of innovative vistas, ideas, thoughts which is to be implemented to make your concept agenda of investment a reality come true. I have found from my practical experience that this small little activity at the dining table will make a great big investment mantra for your family for the next 20 years which will be responsible for sitting relaxed on the dining table for next five decades without any hassles and making out all the luxury available in the family for all the generations to come. Well, this formula is really not that easy but simultaneously it is also not that tough. What all is needed is to give a big boost to the new generation to multiply 15 to 150 in ten years under your guidance and under the control of the elders in the family. My practical experience in dealing and handling with large number of young members of a joint family who are rich and famous has revealed that this formula has brought unprecedented growth of investment in the family because on the one hand a target is fixed for the new generation to be achieved by way of appreciation of the investment while on the other hand complete free hand is being given to do what they like to do. I would suggest all the readers to implement this formula in their family and I would be to very happy to receive from them their success stories in years to come. Do write to me on my direct E-Mail slakhotia@satyam.net.in. I am confident that this simple formula will bring immense fortune in your family due to targeted investment return for which the younger generation will be forced to think of new innovative and new vistas and dynamic style of making money grow by investment in different spheres. Depending upon your money power you can give money to the younger generation to be multiplied in this manner. You can start with just Rs.1 lakh so it becomes Rs.10 1akhs in

10 years and it becomes Rs.100 lakhs in further 10 years. In case you belong to a very rich business family then you should give to the next generation the sum of Rs.15 Crores and let them multiply to Rs.150 Crores in next 10 years and thereafter the final target to be given should be to make this Rs.150 Crores in next 10 years to Rs.1500 Crores. Well, this is the guru mantra of investment to be suggested by you and inspired by you to your next generation for letting money grow under the hands of the next generation.

❑❑❑

36

Buying & Selling of Paintings & Antiques

You are a person of taste. It is time now to make good investment yield and return by buying and selling the items of your taste. You can make your money grow by actively engaging yourself in those items in which you are interested in. For example if you have got interest in antique or if you are interested in painting, then it makes a sense to let painting etc. be part of your investment strategy and encash on your purchase and sale of the paintings by buying at different time and selling the painting to someone who must have it at any cost. This formula will help you to make your investment in painting a good one. It is also time now to consider paintings and antiques as a part of your investment item. One can make good money by actively engaging in the activity of buying and selling the items in which one has got a taste. Hence enjoy and make money, that is the investment mantra for your investment in paintings etc. Once you buy the painting let it be a part of your drawing room which provides you happiness while on the other hand when you like, you sell the paintings for a gain and again make investment in another painting and so the process continues.

❑❑❑

37

Investment in Bank Fixed Deposit

When you are having very small funds at your disposal and you want the safest instrument of investment, then it is time for you to make your investment in Bank Fixed Deposit. Bank Fixed Deposit is definitely known to be a good investment module for all those who want 100 per cent safety and security. However, another important point which must be taken care of is that each Fixed Deposit which you are contemplating to make should be of the value of less than Rs.1 lakh. This matter is of great importance more specifically to small investors who have got small funds available at their disposal. Please remember if your Fixed Deposit is upto Rs.1 lakh, then it is insured and by chance in the event of failure of the bank also, you have not to worry as you are going to get the money in respect of this Fixed Deposit of yours specially because the value is upto Rs.1 lakh. Taking out bank FDR for a duration of five years will also get you a deduction within the overall limit of tax deduction up to Rs 1,50,000 within the total deduction amount under section 80C.

❑❑❑

38

Investment by a Salaried Employee in Property

Are you thinking of buying some commercial property. An office space or a space for godown purpose or a space for a factory, then surely try to make your investment strategy in such a manner that you buy the property by taking maximum loan from bank as well as from friends and relatives. Do remember that if you are buying all these commercial properties specially for letting it out on rent and enjoying a big fixed rental income, then definitely the interest under the provisions of the Income-tax Law is allowed as a deduction while computing your rental income. The special feature is that unlimited deduction is available in respect of the interest on the loan. Hence, whatever be the quantum of the loan, the interest on such loan which has been taken for your investment in the commercial property continues to be fully allowed as a deduction from the rental income so received by you. Also do remember that in the initial years if the rent received is less and interest payment is more, then whatever is the net loss suffered by you, the same will be allowed as a deduction from your any income of the year. For example if rent received is Rs.1 lakh in a year while initially the interest paid is Rs.2.50 lakhs for loan taken for buying the property leaving a net loss of Rs.1.50 1akhs. In this situation this loss of Rs.1.50 1akhs will be allowed set off against even your salary income or from your business income or interest income also. Thus it is good strategy to make the investment in commercial property by taking loans only.

❑❑❑

39

Your Loss in Rented Property is Your Gain

A salaried employee and more specifically and particularly a salaried employee in receipt of house rent allowance as far as possible should never make investment in a residential property in his own name. If a person makes the investment in a residential property in his own name and also makes payment of interest on the loan for the said self-occupied property, in that situation the entire interest payment upto maximum of Rs.2 lakhs per annum will be allowed as a deduction while computing the income of the salaried employee. Now comes the theme that when HRA i.e. House Rent Allowance is received by an employee and specially if he has purchased a house on loan, he enjoys definitely the deduction on loan interest upto Rs.2 lakhs. But the poor fellow will not be able to save even a single penny out of the HRA amount so received by him. Well, for such persons who are in receipt of fixed amount per month by way of House Rent Allowance and they also want to buy a property for self use and stay in the said property, then from investment strategy wise, the best option for investment in the residential house property would have been to buy the property in the name of his spouse or in the name of Hindu Undivided Family and thereafter to take the said property on rent and make payment for rent out of the amount received by way of House Rent Allowance. This investment strategy will help the salaried employee to save lakhs of rupees per annum. Another strategy of investment in residential house property by a person receiving House Rent Allowance would be by way of making investment in the residential house property jointly in the names of self and spouse or self and other members of the family. If the investment is made in this pattern, then it is possible to save income-tax by making payment of House Rent Allowance to the other co-owner of the property thereby the employee receiving the House Rent Allowance can also be a part owner of the property and thus can enjoy deduction by way of interest on loan up to Rs.2 lakhs while on the other hand tax deduction can also be claimed in respect of the payment for House Rent Allowance.

❑❑❑

40

Investment in PPF Account at the beginning the Financial Year

Public Provident Fund Investment can be made by you either in one go or in different installments during the year. You have got full freedom to make the investment in the manner as you like and the amount as you like. However, do ensure that the total contribution or investment during the year in PPF Account does not exceed Rs.1,50,000 in one Financial Year. The best strategy would be to invest in the Public Provident Fund Account right on day one of start of the Financial Year. Hence, wherever possible please try to make investment in the first week itself of April each year in the Public Provident Fund Account which you are maintaining with State Bank of India or with Post Office. Please do remember that the amount which you deposit in the PPF Account enjoys tax deduction under section 80C of the Income-tax Act, 1961 within the overall limit of Rs.1,50,000 lakh. However, it is not necessary that the investment which you make in the PPF Account should come out of the income of the year. Thus, when you make your investment in the PPF Account, the said investment can also come by way of your old saving say of other investment or from any other income or asset which you have got. Do remember the big advantage of your investment in PPF Account in the very first month is that you enjoy the tax deduction on the one hand while you earn higher amount of interest which is tax free. Thus, the tax free interest at the rate of 8.7 per cent per annum acts as a very good incentive for you to make your investment from day one of the Financial Year or as soon as possible after the start of the Financial Year so that you can earn more tax free interest income.

❑❑❑

41

Bank Fixed Deposit Vs Floater Mutual Fund

If you are going to make investment in the Bank Fixed Deposit, then it is worthwhile to have a comparison between your bank Fixed Deposit Investment v. the Investment in the Floater Scheme of the Mutual Fund. Mainly because of the tax related benefits the investment in the Floater Scheme of Mutural Fund may be found to be more efficient in comparison with the investment going to be made by you in the Bank Fixed Deposit. At least there would be 10 to 15 per cent higher yield in comparison with FDR which the Floater Mutual Fund can offer to you.

❑❑❑

42

Mixture of Investments for Section 80C

One of the important investment mantra coupled with tax advantage is that you can make the investment in any one or more mixture of the investments which are available for tax saving under section 80C of the Income-tax Act, 1961 and a special feature is that for making your investment in one or more of these instruments there is no compulsion under the provisions of the Income-tax Law that the money which has been invested for achieving tax deduction under section 80C should come out of the income of the year. Hence, please do remember that you can take out insurance policy with your existing funds or by withdrawing an old investment but still that will enjoy the tax deduction for you. Hence, whenever you like during the whole of the Financial Year, you may make investment in all those items for which tax deduction is permissible under section 80C of the Income-tax Act, 1961 without bothering to find out whether such investment has been made out of the income of the year. Finally, it means that you make the investment which may not be out of the income of the year, still you enjoy the deduction under section 80C of the Income-tax Act, 1961.

❑❑❑

43

Relocation of Your Residential House Property

If you a senior citizen and you find that the present day market value of your residential property has gone up substantially in the last one decade, then right now is the time for you to think of relocation of your residential house property. This investment mantra is applicable if you are owning independent house or a villa of your own or even if you are owning a costly residential apartment in your name. With no current income in tune with the rising cost of living, it is recommended that senior citizens should adopt the investment mantra of relocation of their real estate and plan their investment in such a manner that out of the proceeds received by selling the existing house properly, only 1/3rd amount is invested in buying another residential property in a slightly remote area while 1/3rd of the sale proceeds are invested so as to bring regular income for the senior citizens and finally the balance 1/3rd portion should be so wisely spent in buying capital goods like a car to be maintained with a driver as also other modem gadgets and equipments for the house. From this amount some money may be set aside for meeting family social obligations if any. This type of investment mantra in the form of relocation of your real estate would be really wonderful idea to plan your retirement investment strategy.

❑❑❑

44

Fixed Deposit with a Bank

Before making a Fixed Deposit with a bank, it is time now for you to understand the rules and procedure of the bank and the penalty for withdrawal of the Fixed Deposit amount before the due date. It is always recommended to make not one single Fixed Deposit for a big amount which you would like to invest but to take out small small Fixed Deposits so that even if you have to withdraw on premature basis some amount from the Fixed Deposits, then you don't lose by way of interest etc. Different banks have got different policy regarding calculation of the interest and-some extra amount for premature withdrawal of the bank Fixed Deposit. Hence, whenever you are making any Fixed Deposit with a bank, do always enquire in advance the rules and the procedures for encashment of the Fixed Deposit before the due date. This will help you to earn better yield and good investments in the form of Bank Fixed Deposit.

❑❑❑

45

The Special Tax Deduction from Your Rental Income

You are thinking of having a good source of regular income so as to take care of your day to day expenditure then the best option which is recommended for this purpose is to buy a property and put it on rent. The biggest advantage of making investment in rental housing or renting commercial property is the great big advantage which is available under the Income-tax Law namely the granting of special 30 per cent deduction from the rental amount so received by a tax payer on account of various expenses incurred for repair, maintenance and collection charges of the rented house property. Hence, the net impact of this important deduction is that the maximum rate of income-tax payable by an individual in respect of rental income as a result of the above mentioned 30 per cent deduction would be just 21 per cent only. Hence, even if you are coming in the highest income bracket, even then it makes a sense to buy residential or commercial property and put the same on rent and thereby avail tax rate of maximum 21 per cent only. Apart from maximum tax of 21 per cent on your rental income another hidden advantage is with reference to appreciation of the property in the years to come and also appreciation by way of increase in the rent.

❑❑❑

46

Consolidate Your Real Estate

When you are 50 plus, time now is to get ready for you to adopt the management mantra of consolidating your Real Estate. Yes, it is time now for you to concentrate on consolidating Real Estate owned by you in different parts of India and abroad. As the age increases, the mobility of investment gets reduced. Hence in tune with the same, it is recommended that all individuals above the age of 50 must start the process of consolidation of Real Estate which will bring them peace and happiness and would also provide relief to the future inheritors of the Real Estate from the unnecessary work hassles connected with different Real Estates scattered in different parts of India. Your activity of consolidating Real Estate specially when you are 50 plus will help you reap good fruits of consolidation in the form of saving of your time and energy and taking good care of the Real Estate and other assets because they are now in a consolidated form.

❑❑❑

47

Never buy more than one Residential Property in Your Name

You are owner of one house or one apartment. You have got two sons or two children and you plan to buy out another house property in the back of your mind to ultimately distribute both the properties amongst your two children. Even when such is the theme of buying the second residential house property, please do remember that from tax angle, it makes no sense at all to buy the second house property in your name. Under the provisions of Income-tax Act, 1961 the second house property if purchased by you in your name with your fund and is occupied by you or any other family member of yours, then under the provisions of the said Income-tax Law, there will be liability by way of deemed rental income from the second house property. Well, it appears to be ridiculous statement for most investors but the fact remains that under the Income-tax Law, there is no income-tax liability in respect of the first house property owned by you which is used for residential purpose. While if you own the second house property which is self occupied and which is not earning any rental income, still based on the provisions contained in the said Income-tax Act, the deemed rental income in respect of the second house property will be added to your income thereby increasing your income-tax liability.

Hence, the good investment mantra is that never buy second house property in the name of that person who is already owner of one residential house property. Well, you can now think of different family members in whose names to buy the second residential house property and avoid being taxed on the rental income which actually you have not received: Finally, from the income-tax perspective it is now a very important investment mantra never never to buy or own more than one residential property for self occupation in one's own name.

❑❑❑

48

Investment in Real Estate

If you want to make money in Real Estate, it is time for you now to buy old house, renovate it extensively and sell it off. This type of money making idea is very much popular in USA and the same can be replicated in Indian context also. The next time if you come across some property which is in a dilapitated condition, then it would make a sense to buy that property and then renovate it with the ultimate objective of selling it away.

❑❑❑

49

Stay Attached in the Stock Market

Watch out regularly the statistics of the Stock Market Sensex which will inspire you to invest more in the equity and thereby make your money grow. For example the Sensex Returns in percentage for the Financial Year ending 31st March 2007 was 15.9 per cent while for the Financial Year ending 31st March 2008 it was 19.7 per cent. But in the Financial Year ending on 31st March 2009 the Sensex Returns show a negative figure of minus 37.9 per cent but finally again during the Financial Year ending 31st March 2010 the Sensex Returns were 80.5 per cent. Thus, a review of the statistics from time to time will really inspire you to carry out investments in the stock market and make your money grow. However, to achieve the best results, one must stay attached in the stock market for a minimum period of three years. Supposing you invested in benchmark index fund a the start of FY2006 and remained invested till the end of FY15, your returns at the end of the 10 year period would be 331%. Hence invest with long term perspective.

❑❑❑

50

Never Worry about What will happen to the Investment in Years to Come

Never ever worry about your investment specially with regard to what will happen of the investment in the years to come. Well, this is very important investment mantra whereby the message which is proposed to be given to all the readers is that they should never ever worry about the future plus side or minus side of the investment which they have made today. This principle would hold good for the Real Estate sector as well as the stock market. You might buy a particular piece of property and then a month later you hear about excess supply in the area and that you start worrying about the likelihood of market value going down of your Real Estate. Well, don't worry at all. Yes, however, before making the investment always very carefully watch out the pros and cons and then make your jump into the investment but having once made the investment, don't just grumble over the situation and never worry about the likelihood depreciation of the value of your investment. Do remember that investment is not to be made for a day or a month but it is a long time affair. A small little turbulance should not affect your investment strategy otherwise it may lead you into selling out the Real Estate or other investments at a loss. Similar would also be the situation with regard to the stock market. If you make investment in some new issues after carefully making a study of the issue and then suddenly you find that just after listing the market value of the stock had depreciated by more than 10 per cent and then you are worried and tensed. Immediately you might think of even selling out that stock but this type of hasty decision will not be good for your investment health.

❑❑❑

51

Never buy Agricultural Land with Patta

Never buy agricultural land with a *patta*. Generally speaking when you want to go in for your investment in agricultural land, you are just happy and relaxed as soon as your work relating to real estate is completed on your agricultural land. However, one very important point which must be taken into consideration is that you should never buy agricultural land with a *patta* on it. The agricultural land which has got a *patta* means that it is a lease given for cultivation to some another person. The impact would be drastic reduction in the market value of the agricultural land which you have purchased. Hence, in the agricultural land which you are going to purchase if that happens to be an existing *patta* (lease given to another person for carrying out agricultural operations), then make sure that in the first place you get that *patta* cancelled and thereafter get the *patta* consideration recorded in the office of patwari and finally when the sale deed is executed, do mention that on the said agricultural land there is no *patta* to any person. Finally in the sale deed which you are executing also take special care to get existing *patta* holder as a witness in the sale deed to make your paper work really strong.

❑❑❑

52

Projected Cash Flow Chart for Raising Your Child

If you are going to have a baby, plan now, save and invest wisely. Prepare a projected cash flow chart of the total expenditure required for raising a child born to you. Also prepare in this chart all that expenditure which will be required based on today's expenses sheet coupled with inflation for the future years. Thus, the chart should be prepared for all such amount which will be required before your junior baby heads off to college. Your insurance planning and liquid money planning will be required to be geared up in tune with the changed circumstances and situations specially when you are having a baby. Advance planning before having a baby is needed in the form of saving, saving and saving and investing, investing and investing so as to have a better combination of good funds flow without any hassles at a time when the baby is born in your family.

❑❑❑

53

Must Save 25% of Your Income for Rainy Day

Every prudent investor must save 25 per cent of his income for the rainy day. This is one of the very important investment mantra to be implemented into action by a small as well as a big investor. 'Rain rain go away, come again another day, little Johny wants to play.' This is what you must have been reading in your nursery class. This is exactly what your father was reading when he was in nursery and finally today you see you children and also your grand children reading the same nursery rhyme. This nursery rhyme has got great bearing on the investment strategy for all ages to come. Rain will come. You cannot stop it. But if you save money for that rainy day, then surely it would be wonderful investment strategy from your side. Hence, even if you are in difficult time today and you find it big problem to manage your both ends meet, even then it is strongly recommended that you should save at least 25 per cent of your income for the rainy day. This saving formula if implemented by you today will make you live in the wonderland of great happiness as you march ahead in your fulfilling of your golden mantra.

❑❑❑

54

Time to Invest in Term Insurance Policy

It is time now for you to take out a term policy of insurance so as to avoid any tension to the family members in the event of untimely mishap on the one hand while on the other hand the liability continues after death of a family members. Still for home loan the liability continues. For car loan the liability continues and the liability also continues for education loan if any taken by you for the family member. The best investment strategy for taking out term insurance policy is to make a total of all the loans from banks, financial institutions as well as from the employer and once the sum total of all the loans and liability is prepared, then just add 25 per cent of the loan amount and then take out a Term Insurance Policy. For example if total loans for house, for car, for education etc. of Mr. A comes to Rs.40 lakhs, then the investment strategy should be to take out the Term Insurance Policy for Rs.50 1akhs. If the term insurance policy is taken in this manner, then it will be possible to take care of settling down all the existing loans and advances and liabilities on the one hand while it will also go to make some available money for the family. Hence, one can protect the family by spending money on taking out term insurance and the amount spent on your investment in the form of term insurance will definitely give you unprecedented peace of mind and tension free living because all calamities resulting into financial breakdown of the family have been taken care of mainly because of the term insurance policy.

❑❑❑

55

Invest in Fixed Maturity Insurances Plan

For taking care of big liability in the future which might arise as a result of proposed marriage of your daughter or higher education of your children the investment strategy should be to take out insurance policy with a Fixed Maturity Plan and such Maturity Plan should coincide with the projected marriage year of your daughter or the projected time for money requirement for the education of your children. Hence, focused and planned investment should be made in insurance policies so that the investment in insurance premium brings home the money required at the desired time.

❑❑❑

56

Don't buy Car on Installment Plan

You want to invest money in buying a car, You have got a bank Fixed Deposit also. With your pay slip or Income-tax Return your bankers are easily willing to lend you money for buying the car on installment. You are in a fix. You do not know whether to buy the car with down payment by withdrawing the money from the bank Fixed Deposit or in the alternative let the bank Fixed Deposit go up earning interest income for you and you make purchase of the car under Installment Plan by making monthly installments of the car payment. In such a situation before jumping into any decision, the best answer would be to calculate the impact of net income inflow and the net outflow in respect of both the transactions namely the transaction of interest income to be received on bank Fixed Deposit interest as well the transaction involving outflow in the form of payment of interest to the bank or other financial institution for buying the car. Generally speaking it would be advisable to withdraw your bank Fixed Deposit and make down payment of the car in comparison with continuing your bank Fixed Deposit and also continuing your car loan. The main theme is because of the interest inflow and outflow. In most cases it would therefore, be worthwhile to buy the car by withdrawing your bank FDR because your bank Fixed Deposit gives you a yield much lower in comparison with bank interest which you are required to pay in respect of the car purchased for self occupation in particular. The answer again in most cases would be in favour of dismantling your bank Fixed Deposit and going in for down payment of the car more specifically if you are buying the car for self occupation only and with no business income. The main reason is because of the fact that if you continue to maintain your bank Fixed Deposit, then the interest in respect of the said bank Fixed Deposit would be added to your income and you would be called upon to make payment of income-tax at the applicable tax rate. Supposing you are coming within the maximum marginal rate bracket, then 30 per cent of your income from the bank Fixed Deposit interest would just be melted away in making payment of income-tax thereby bringing lower net yield on your investment in the said bank Fixed Deposit. Similarly, when you start comparing the interest which you pay on the car loan you find that the said interest is not allowed as a deduction to you specially when you are a salaried employee or a retired person having no income from business or profession. Do make your investment in car out of the withdrawal of your funds which are yielding lower interest in comparison with the interest which you pay on the car EMI to the bank.

❑❑❑

57

Investment in Zero Coupon Bonds

It is a good time now to get your money ready for investment in the Ten Year Discount Bond of the Rural Electrification Corporation Limited (REC) popularly known as Zero Coupon Bond in the Income-tax Terminology. The Ministry of Finance vide its notification dated 8th April 2010 has notified the Zero Coupon Bonds of REC to be issued for ten years. These bonds will be issued on or before 31st Day of March 2011. The amount which will be paid by REC at maturity or at redemption of the bond would Rs. 30000 for each bond. The period of life of the bond will be for ten years only. Hence, keeping in view of the tax advantages which are available in respect of the Zero Coupon Bond it is worthwhile for the individual tax payers to plan their investment right now in these bonds for reaping efficient, intelligent investment plan. The fact that the permission has been granted by the Government to Rural Electrification Corporation to issue 25 lakh bonds itself speaks about the importance and the popularity of these bonds. Watch out for more details in the newspaper about the timing when these bonds would be available for sale. But definitely it is good investment tool for the investment which you want to block in for ten long year period.

❑❑❑

58

Monthly Cash Flow Chart – A must for you

Prepare your monthly cash flow chart and then plan your investment strategy. Never proceed to make the investment or to incur heavy expenditure without first preparing your monthly cash flow chart. Do remember that monthly preparation of your cash flow chart enables you to have proper combination of the spending as well as saving your funds and then you are sure never to have the problem of cash crunch. Once you plan and manage your cash flow chart it is even worthwhile to make preparation of forthcoming projected cash flow chart to enable you to plan the investment strategy of your investment in tune with the spending strategy for the months to follow.

❑❑❑

59

Invest Liberally in Commercial Property

Invest in more than one commercial property direct in your name because there is no hassle with regard to your investment in commercial property. Hence, invest as much as you like directly in your name itself and own as many commercial properties you want to hold because there is no liability to wealth tax at all in respect of your investments made in the commercial properties.

❑❑❑

60

Wealth Tax Exemption on Unlimited Residential Properties given on Rent

Residential property you have owned a very big one and you are aware that it is exempt from wealth tax. But now you want to buy more than one residential property and your investment in more than one residential property in your name should not attract any wealth tax liability. Well this is your investment dream. But to achieve the same what is required to ensure that the entire investment in more than one residential properties are made for the purpose of letting it out for more than 300 days in a year. Hence, if you own more than one residential properties, houses, villas, apartments in your own name but each of them is given on rent for more than 300 days in a year, then the big advantage of your investment is that you are not required to make payment of any wealth tax at all. Yes, this is true, because the provisions of the wealth tax law gives full exemption in respect of all the properties which are residential in nature owned by you if they are put on rent for more than 300 days in a year. However, on and from the financial year 2015-16 the Wealth-tax has been abolished.

❑❑❑

61

Invest in Capital Gain Bonds

Generally all those persons who derive long-term capital gains specially on selling their immovable property go in for investment in capital gain bonds up to the maximum value of Rs.50 lakhs because the investment in capital gain bonds make available for you tax concession or tax exemption in respect of the tax payable by you on your long-term capital gain. It may be recalled here that under the Income tax law one can make investment up to Rs.50 lakhs in capital gain bonds issued by NHAI or REC and that this investment made in the bonds gets deducted from the capital gain amount so accruing to the assessee. These bonds carry interest of approximately 5 per cent per annum. The interest so received is also not tax exempt and is taxable. Knowing the salient features of the capital gain bonds it, therefore, makes a sense in many cases for the tax payers not to make the investment in the capital gain bonds rather to make payment of the capital gains tax liability of 20 per cent in respect of long-term capital gains accruing to the assessee and the balance amount after making payment of the tax may be invested in any fruitful investment option specially for all those tax payers who are able to make money of 15 to 18 per cent per annum on their money if made available to them. Hence, if you feel that you can earn anything between 15 to 18 per cent per annum on your money then you should definitely not go in making investment in capital gain bonds just to save Income-tax. For example if you are in business and just suppose that out of the capital gains amount of Rs.50 lakhs you make payment of tax on this amount of capital gain amounting to Rs.10 lakhs leaving a net amount of Rs. 40 lakhs surplus available with you. Now you have to yourself answer that with this Rs. 40 lakhs available at your disposal how many times in a year you can circulate it in your business and earn heavy profit on the same. For most persons who are business people it therefore makes a sense to make payment of the capital gain and not to go in for investment in capital gain bonds and the net resultant figure after payment of the capital gain tax should be so invested that bring home more yield because the surplus money is put to business. The dictum therefore is never invest in capital gain bonds, better pay tax and use the balance money in your business or for buying some attractive Real Estate. The net money supply in your family will be much higher if we compare the return on your capital gains money deducting therefrom the tax liability. However, if you are not in a position to make 15 per cent or 18 per cent income generation on the money available with you, then there is, no option but to go in for investment in capital gain bonds. The long and the short of the capital gain bonds is that before jumping immediately to make the investment in these bonds, it is time for you now to think in advance about the projected calculation of the net money available at your disposal after three years had you deposited the money in capital gain bonds and compare this amount with the net projected amount of money to be made available with you after three years after you have made the tax payment and utilized the money for earning higher income. My practical experience is that if you invest the money in some good lucrative Real Estate after suffering the capital gain tax today, it is definitely worthwhile to do away with your investment of capital gain bonds and better to pay the tax and receive ultimately higher profits.

❑❑❑

62

Invest in Insurance Policy and Mutual Fund Units

You want insurance cover for your family and you also want Mutual Fund Investment. Hence you take a decision to invest in ULIP (Unit Link Insurance Plan) whereby you take out a simple Life Insurance Policy for yourself and the Insurance Company makes the investment of your funds in taking out Insurance Policy thereby making the investment in Mutual Fund Units also. Well, to achieve the best results it is recommended that if you want insurance for your family, better take a specific insurance policy and similarly when you want the investment in Mutual Fund also take out very simple Mutual Fund.

❑❑❑

63

Car Loan with Interest on Reducing Balance

When you want investment in the car and you do not have sufficient money to buy the car on down payment basis, then the only alternative left with you is to buy the car by taking a loan from the bank or from some other financial institution. The important point while taking the car loan or any other loan for that purpose is to carefully screen between the two different set of proposals of loan offered to you by the bank or financial institution: Firstly, the bank may give you the option of granting you car loan with a fixed rate of interest on reducing balance method while the another option may be of granting loan to you at very low rate of interest. Definitely the proposal to charge very low rate of interest may look to be lucrative. But it is charged without considering the reduced amount of the loan. Hence, when the option is available to you for taking the car loan, do compare the fixed rate of interest versus the floating rate of interest, only then take the decision as to which course is beneficial to you. Generally speaking it will be better if you opt for the scheme of charging interest on the reducing balance which will definitely be more rewarding and would be more cost efficient in the long run.

❑❑❑

64

Joint Business with Friends and Relatives

When you get your retirement benefits, it is time for you now before planning your investments to. say a very big no to your friends and relatives. It is very common that as soon as the person receives big fat amount in respect of his retirement benefits, a big team of relatives, well wishers and friends are there ready without your call to give you suggestions and answers to park your funds in the most profitable manner. Some of the relatives may also come up with the proposal of joint business to be done with your money and their hard work. Well, the best answer for all these problems is definitely to say a big no to all your friends and relatives specially when big money is going to come to you.

❑❑❑

65

Don't Come too close to Your Spouse for Investment

A practical life investment mantra specially for the just married young couples. Don't ever come too much close to your spouse as far as your investment matters are concerned. Well, this tip may not bring acceptance to many young persons who have just been married but still this tip remains the most important tip mainly for young couples who have just being married. So, go slowly with your spouse specially with regard to the aspects connected with sharing of the information in investments and telling your spouse all about your investment. Your slow action will be ultimately good for you in the years to come. Why, when and how just don't ask these questions. Only follow this investment mantra.

❑❑❑

66

Investment Chart of Your Family for Movable and Immovable Properties

Prepare investment chart of your family in respect of all your movable and immovable investments. If you want to live a hassle free, tension free life, then definitely this chart should be kept handy. Also the contents of this chart should be known to all adult members in the family. With reference to the chart for immovable property, care should be to write down in the chart the legal status of the property whether there is a lease hold property or a free hold property and whether the property has been registered in the office of sub-registrar or is only on power of attorney. All these details if mentioned exhaustively in the investment chart, then it will help you to plan your investment in a more befitting manner.

❑❑❑

67

Reverse Mortgage for Senior Citizens

If you are a senior citizen with less current income but big house property, then it is time now for you to resort to reverse mortgage. Large number of senior citizens are there in the country located in different parts of India who are in their own palacial building or in apartments, the market value of this building or apartments due to the passage of time is very costly because there has been overall appreciation in the value of the property. If we compare the purchase price and the today's market value of the property, then in many cases there is hundred times difference. Well, it is time to celebrate the appreciation of your property but the problem is appreciation is there but there is no current income and that due to rising inflation in the country meeting both hands is becoming difficult day by day specially for all those persons with fixed income. Hence, to achieve the best results one option for such a person would have been to sell the property. Well, this idea is not suitable to you. If we talk about selling the property then such persons may feel that their status in the society will get lost if they sell this property and move out in some location. Besides there are innumerable hassles, problems and tensions in the selling of the property and buying another small property. Well, the best golden mantra for this category of persons is not to sell their property but only to have a reverse mortgage of their property. This is wonderful great idea with no hassles and no tension and no much paper work and no much botheration also. All you have to do is to go to your Bank and ask the banker to give the details concerning reverse mortgage. Under the concept of reverse mortgage the senior citizens in particular can take advance or loan by mortgaging their property. The best part of the situation is that all senior citizen will have no obligation to make payment of loan amount so taken by mortgage. Likewise, if the property is mortgaged under this concept of reverse mortgage, it is not treated as a sale. Hence any amount received from the bank under this innovative concept of reverse mortgage will not be treated as the income of the assessee and that there is no liability to capital gain tax also. Therefore, resorting to the concept of reverse mortgage is really very interesting mainly for senior citizens. Ultimately after the demise of the owner the property goes to the legal heir or all the persons who have been named in Will and finally that person settles the bank loan and takes over the property. Thus good life style can be achieved even by persons with no much income by taking advantage of this concept of reverse mortgage.

❑❑❑

68

Regular Investment Introspection

For achieving the best result for your investment it is time now to have a regular investment introspection. It is recommended that every half year one should have introspection in respect of all the assets. This introspection should become a part of regular and routine work of yours. Do have the introspection of movable as well as the immovable assets and investments owned by you. Just like we have the health check up camp, in the same manner it is worthwhile to think of having investment introspection activity at least every six months.

❑❑❑

69

Sell Investments as per Your Target

Fix the target and sell your investments should be your important motto in dealing with the investments made by you. What is your current target is not the point to be discussed. But what is relevant is that in your own frame of mind think what will make you happy if you sell that particular asset at what rate and in respect of movable asset like equity if you are happy when the stock appreciates by 50 per cent, then have the need of selling the stock as soon as its market value exceeds 50 per cent of the investment. Reversely you may have the very ambitious appreciation target of minimum 100 per cent and supposing you are able to achieve 100 per cent appreciation in the value of your shares, let us say after 9 months from the date of investment, then surely you must at this point of time sell the shares and not be too much greedy. Similar would also be the situation with regard to your investment in movable properties. You may buy a property and you set your target that I will sell the property only when there is 200 per cent appreciation in the value of my investment. As soon as you achieve the said target, you should then sell that investment. The theme is that judiciously and cautiously fix up the target which you want to achieve by way of appreciation in the value of the investment made by you and once you have-achieved the target, it is time now for you to sell that asset.

❑❑❑

70

Squeeze Your Expenses and Save

In the coming downturn the best investment theme would be to cut down on your expenses. It is time now to squeeze your expenses on day to day basis and also squeeze the expenses on the luxury. And finally let wasteful expenses be out from your budget. By cutting down on useless expenses, try to save something and a small little saving would be worth, a big benefit for you specially in all that economic downturn period.

❑❑❑

71

Small is Beautiful

Small is beautiful. This is what Mother Teresa used to say always. What Mother Teresa used to say is a reality in the spiritual world as also in the investment world. Taking inspiration from the quotation of Mother Teresa think of making a small investment in the Public Sector Undertaking shares which are offered to the small investors at a discounted price of say 5 per cent. Achieve the benefit and the advantage of buying shares at a lower price specially when such shares are offered at a discount to the small investors. Grab it is a small mantra for you and everyone in the family. When you make the investment in such shares, try to make it a point to apply for new shares in the names of all family members so that you are able to get good allotment but for this purpose the first point which always should be kept handy is to open the Demat Account for every family member. Keep ready the Demat Account of every family member and then you go to make your money on your investment in the shares specially of PSU organizations where many times the shares are offered at a discount to the small investors.

❑❑❑

72

Investments in Foreign Country

It is also time now to think of investment in foreign country away from the shores of India because now a great opportunity is available to every investor to make the investment outside India. Investing in foreign country is hassle free now a days. The restrictions concerning Foreign Exchange Management Act now a days are very very few as far as the investment is concerned in a foreign country. In every financial year you can invest up to US $ 2.5 lakhs per individual in any foreign country. Thus, it is time for you now to plan your investment in foreign country. Before making investment in the foreign country do make sure about the rules and the regulations concerning investment and the taxation aspects in the foreign country. Generally speaking the investment in foreign country takes place mainly in respect of real estate and also certain shares of different listed companies. When it comes to real estate, before entering into a final deal, make sure that the title is crystal clear. Similarly, when you are making your investment in shares, do take care to find that the charges of brokerage etc. are reasonable and that you compare the prevailing purchase price by reference to the news appearing on the television or the rate printed in the newspaper. When we talk of foreign investment now generally no investment by Indian is made in a foreign country in investment options like the bank Fixed Deposit and the bonds etc. The rate of yield on the investment in Bank Fixed Deposit and bonds in a foreign country is much lower. Hence; it makes no sense to make investment by way of bank FDR in a foreign country or to buy bonds of the foreign company or country. By proper planning substantial money can be invested in foreign country in the names of different family members because each individual is permitted to take away up to US $ 2.5 lakhs every year to make foreign investment. For more details visit the website of Reserve Bank of India and have a look at the provisions contained in Foreign Exchange Management Act.

❑❑❑

73

Investment in New Public Issues

New Public Issue coming up of very good and reputed companies of Public Sector Undertakings, then it is definitely a time for making investment in this type of IPO. However, your problem is you do not have ready cash available at your disposal to make the investment in this new IPO. It is a wonderful time in such situation to get married to the shares being issued in the IPO by taking a loan from the bank. For best results let the shares remain for a long time. Also do remember that all family members should invest in the new issue which according to you is very good specially even after taking loan from the bank. Please do remember that the interest on loan which you pay to make your investment in the new issue of the shares, this interest will be allowed as a deduction while computing your short term capital gain in particular specially if you are contemplating to sell the shares in less than one year's time.

❑❑❑

74

Invest in Chit Fund Scheme

If you are in business, then it makes a sense for you to invest in Chit Fund Scheme. However, do ensure that the Chit Fund Scheme in which you invest should not be Cheat Fund. Hence, carefully examine the credentials of the Chit Fund Operator and only then take a decision to make the investment in the Chit Fund. Taking out a Chit and receiving the money from the Chit Fund may help you to take care of your temporary financial problems. Also do remember that under the Income-tax Law in respect of your investment in the Chit Fund no amount of income is taxable. Similarly no amount of loss is deductible and similarly no deduction is permissible on the investment in the fund.

❑❑❑

75

Money Making Mantra for Your children

Money making mantra for your children and more particularly your minor children should also be one important item of agenda in your diary. You make money. You know where to invest. Good, but the point is it is also time now to explain the money making mantra to your young minor children in particular. Take little time from your busy schedule to explain the importance of money and savings to your children. To achieve the best results, purchase a small box and give it to your each child. Let children develop the habit of putting coin a day in this box. Every month let the amount from this box be withdrawn, your child should now sit down with you and count the money and then take your child to the bank and let this monthly small or big amount whatever it be invested by way of deposit in the bank account and now let the child maintain details of monthly amount deposited in the bank account on a piece of paper. Six months later bring the pass books from the bank and let the child understand how the money has grown by way of interest in respect of the money which he has deposited in the bank. If you are able to develop the art of making money in your young children right now, then definitely you will find that your children would be great investors in the years to come and that their habit of wasting money will also be cut down.

❑❑❑

76

Investment in Industrial Plot

Investment for industrial plot should be made in upcoming areas. The best is to make investment in Industrial Estates developed by the State Government. While you want to take the best from the Industrial Estate, try to select such Industrial Estate which has got extra advantages attached to it in comparison with other surrounding Industrial Estates. Always compare the adjoining areas of Industrial Estates. Only then take a decision. For example in Rajasthan at Nimrana the Industrial Estate has come up very beautifully. It is also known as a Japanese Industrial Estate. A separate zone of land has been demarcated exclusively for industries to be set up by Japanese companies. Likewise the new freight corridor and the KMP on the outskirts of Delhi would make your investment very fruitful specially if you are looking at buying a land for industrial use. Near Nimrana a new Industrial Estate will shortly be developed by RICO which will provide many more investment vistas for profitable gain specially because it is situated within the distance of 5 to 7 kms. from Nimrana and is also connected by rail. Thus, think of Industrial Estate investment looking to the advantages offered by the State and also other connected locational advantages.

❑❑❑

77

Buying a Property with Loan to be Let Out

When you are interested to make investment for purchasing property with the ultimate aim of letting it out on rent so as to have a fixed rental income, the investment mantra is to buy such property as far as possible by taking loan. This loan can be taken from banks, any other financial institutions and a friend or a relative etc. The special feature which would make your investment very rewarding is that the entire interest without any upper limit would be allowed as a deduction in respect of interest paid for buying a property which is put on rent. This principle would apply for investment in commercial property or residential property or the industrial property.

❑❑❑

78

In Whose Name to buy Factory Land

When you are contemplating to buy the factory land, as far as possible do not buy the- factory land in the name of the person who is going to own the factory and will be going to run the factory. This is really very important matter. The best investment mantra would be to buy the land in the names of some of the family members so that ultimately the land which is purchased by the family members is given on rent or lease to the factory which is to be run there. The advantage in this concept of buying the factory land is that had the factory land being purchased by the company running the factory, then it would not have got any deduction by way of depreciation. This is because of the fact that the Income-tax Law specifically prohibits grant of depreciation on land. Hence, if the land is purchased in the names of some of the family members and in turn is given on rent to the business entity carrying on the running of the factory, then the rent so paid by the factory would be allowed as a deduction to them while for the person receiving the rent it would be income which would be taxable subject to deduction of all expenses incurred in letting out the property on rent including the expense by way of interest on land.

❑❑❑

79

Form a Private Equity Fund

If you want to make money on your investment, it is time now for you to combine together and form a Private Equity Fund. Yes, Private Equity Fund is the shape of things to come. Presently it is only operational in a big manner all over the world but in India this concept is comparatively new. Hence, all those who are interested to make money grow should surely try to form a Private Equity Fund with the aim of investing in the upcoming start up business organizations of fresh business people. It is also worthwhile to think of setting up an Enterprise Fund which can be specifically demarcated for money to be given for starting a new small enterprise by young entrepreneurs who have just passed out from college. Some of the MBA Institutes should be visited and the young entrepreneurs who have just completed their studies in MBA should be encouraged to start their own business enterprise with the funds being provided by the Private Equity Fund or the Entrepreneur Fund. For this purpose the best option would be to set up a Limited Liability Partnership comprising of five or ten or more than that friends who can pull in their resources together to start this business venture of helping the young entrepreneurs thereby making entrepreneurship increase in the country on the one hand while on the other hand make their income and wealth grow. The Government has now provided certain tax concessions in the sphere of investments in REITS etc.

❑❑❑

80

Sovereign Gold Bonds 2015-16

The Government has brought out a very interesting Scheme for the investors in the form of Sovereign Gold Bonds 2015-16. These Bonds will be restricted for sale to resident Indian entities including individuals, HUFs, Trusts, Universities and to the Charitable institutions. The minimum limit of investment in these Bonds is 2 Grams while the maximum limit of investment is 500 Grams per annum. The investment can be made by only Resident Indians. Thus, a Non-Resident Indian cannot make investment in these Bonds. The date of receipt of bond will be the same which is inscribed on the holding certificate. These Bonds can be issued in Demat Format or in Physical Format. Thus, both the Formats of the Bonds will be valid in law. The Government is also going to pay interest at the rate of 2.25 per cent per annum and the same will be exempted from tax. The interest will be calculated on half yearly basis and will be served directly into the account mentioned in the application form or in the Account linked with the Demat Account.

The Post Maturity Interest will not be payable. The information on these Bonds further states that it is mandatory for the investors to provide bank account details to facilitate payment of interest/.maturity value.

As regards the nomination facility it is provided that the sole Holder or all the joint Holders may nominate one or more persons as nominee.

The maturity period of all Sovereign Gold Bonds will be 8 years from the date of issue. The investor can go in for premature redemption on the coupon dates from the 5th year of issuance.

These Bonds would be tradable on exchanges of NDS which shall be notified in due course. The special feature of these Bonds is that the holders of the Sovereign Gold Bonds shall be entitled to create pledge, hypothecation or lien in favour of scheduled banks.

The application form for these Sovereign Gold Bonds is available at all the scheduled commercial bank branches and at the designated Post Offices only. It is really a good tool of investment in the present scenario specially if you are possessing old and out of date jewellery which can be converted into these Bonds. The fact remains that this Gold Bond Scheme is going to be a big hit. In the first lot itself 63,000 applications for almost 250 crores have been received. I feel that "Sovereign Gold Bonds" would be good investment Tool specially because some interest will also be a granted on these Bonds which would be tax free.

❑❑❑

81

Where do I go to buy Gold

When you are contemplating to buy gold, then immediately you find the most easy way to buy the gold is from your bank. It is true that buying gold from your banker has many advantages. The first and most important advantage is that as a buyer you can be sure that you are genuinely buying a 24 carat gold. However, there is one very big disadvantage. This big disadvantage is in the form of higher purchase price. Yes, if you buy the gold from the banks, the banks would generally charge around 5 to 10 per cent higher than the market price for the gold when they sell to their customers. Hence, if you are contemplating to make big investment in gold, then surely you should not buy the gold from your bank. It is also possible for you to take delivery of the gold through Commodity Exchanges like Multi Commodity Exchange popularly known as MCX and National Commodity and Derivative Exchange commonly known as MCDEX. Both these Exchanges have gold trading contract and different sizes for the convenience of the investors. As per the concept of buying gold from these exchanges, the investors can take delivery of the pure gold either in the Demat Account opened for this purpose or if required physical delivery of the gold can also be taken. The brokerage in these two exchanges is generally very very low in comparison to the brokerage being charged by the bank. These exchanges charge brokerage of around 0.25 per cent. In case you are contemplating to purchase gold through the Commodity Exchanges, then you are also required to pay nominal warehousing charges still buying the gold is much better and convenient if purchased through the exchanges.

❑❑❑

82

Investment in Non-Traditional Assets

The changing trend in respect of investments has changed recently where we find that the investors more particularly the new young investors having started making investment in non-traditional assets. The non-traditional investment would be in making investment in rare coins, stamps and also fine wine. These investments are going to bring a big fortune to the investors in the forthcoming one decade from now. In western country many billionaiers are these days making investments in non-traditional assets mentioned above. In the next one decade we could very well see the unprecedented rise of investment in these tangible assets. Prudent investors should carefully think of making investment in these rare items because the future is bright. For example the world over the stamp market presently is US $ 10 billion in a year. There is also an index dedicated to stamps known as SG 100 Index which is updated monthly. Many operators even have a concept of Guaranteed Minimum Return Contract (GMRC) whereby they offer investor at least 15 per cent return on their investment or 50 per cent appreciation over ten years. Similarly in U.K. a very popular investment fund namely Premier Cru is very actively engaged in the Wine Investment Fund.

❑❑❑

83

You may avoid ULIPs

Recently a newspaper headline said that the investors should avoid ULIPS because the murky cocktail of insurance and investment involves high costs and it is very difficult for a normal investor to understand the terms and conditions and rules of these ULIPS. Generally ULIPS can be redeemed after three years but it definitely makes a sense to remain invested for a very very long term. One cannot make a differentiation in two separate schemes of ULIPS. Hence, the retail investor generally would not be able to compare two different ULIP Plans. Another newspaper report further says that Indians are reluctant to invest in Mutual Funds on fears of high risk and lack of information on how the investment product works.

❑❑❑

84

Investment in Time Share Resorts

Many people make investment in time share resorts. The objective of investment in time share resorts is to take advantage for a fixed number of years of the various properties owned by the time share company. Generally people find it very convenient to be a part of time share and thereby also take advantage of staying in time share property at different locations. It has been seen that most of the persons who have invested in time share properties do not find their investment a very lucrative investment in the years to come. This is mainly because of the fact that yearly maintenance charges have to be paid by the owner of the time share property. These charges keep on increasing year after year and thereby they put a financial burden on the investor who has invested the money in the time share property. It is, therefore, worthwhile not to go in for investment in time share property but to go in for taking holidays based on special offers available in the newspapers. It is well known fact that these days innumerable good offers keep on pouring at regular intervals in various newspapers dealing with holidays being made available at a comparatively cheaper price. These days even foreign holidays are being made affordable for the common man. Still if you wish to make investment in the time share property, then before making investment do take care to select the best in the market to avoid any problems at a future point of time.

❑❑❑

85

Partnership Deed & Succession Planning

All those persons who have invested their money in the partnership firm should carefully note down one very important investment mantra which will be of importance to them at some point of time in their life. It is well known fact that generally in the partnership deed details are written about the names and addresses of different partners, the name of the business enterprise, the profit sharing ratio, the capital contribution as also the details about interest on capital. The partnership deed may also contain details regarding management of day to day affairs of the firm as also operation of the bank account. Thus, all the above mentioned pointers are simple and routine items which are contained in every partnership deed. However, from the point of view of investment and for safeguarding the investment in the partnership firm for the years to come, it is strongly recommended that your partnership deed must contain a very specific clause about continuance of the partnership firm in the event of death of some partners. Well, if nothing is written in the partnership deed on the death of any one of the partner, generally it is seen that whatever is the balance lying to the credit of the partner is paid to the legal heir of the partner. Now the important question which generally comes to our mind is whether on the happening of death of one of the partners his legal heir or his spouse would be taken in the partnership firm. This aspect is really very important even for joint family businesses as also for the partnership entered between two friends who are non-relatives. From the point of investment strategy, it is recommended that your partnership deed should contain clear cut guidelines on the terms and conditions settled amongst the partners with special reference to succession of the partners share in the partnership firm consequent to his death or retirement. This important and small point will definitely help a large number of families to avoid hassles and tensions in the event of death of a family member who is a partner in the partnership firm. The above mentioned investment tip would equally be relevant as far as the limited liability partnership firm of business is concerned. Hence, whether it is the partnership firm or the limited liability partnership, in both the situations care should be taken while drafting the partnership deed to specifically mention the details and the action plan in the event of demise of any of the partners.

❑❑❑

86

SIP - Systematic Investment Planning

SIP – Systematic Investment Planning specially in Mutual Funds is strongly recommended to take care of the rising stock market as well as the falling stock market because the SIP route enables you to do your investment in a particular Mutual Fund. Hence, if you adopt the concept of Systematic Investment Plan of a Mutual Fund, you find no hassles and no tension with regard to the investment which you are making because even if the market goes very bullish, you do not have much to regret. Supposing today the stock market happens to be at rock bottom, a question might arise in the minds of the investors whether we should make the investment right now in a big way in this market specially in the Mutual Fund. Well, the answer may be no because it is possible that after your investment, the stock market may take a further dip. In that situation the concept of Systematic Investment Planning, it would be better for you to average out your acquisition price because the best advantage of SIP is that every month while you are making investment in the Mutual Fund, you are not affected by the ups and downs of the stock market. A person who plays in the Stock Market has just his average costing by constantly buying and selling the stocks depending upon the prevailing market price. But if you adopt to the concept of SIP, this activity is being done automatically. Hence, even if you are a small investor or a new investor, then surely it makes a sense for you right now to adopt the concept of Systematic Investment Planning in the Mutual Fund. Take out a fixed amount every month to be invested under the Systematic Investment Plan of the Mutual Fund. You can start your activity with 1000 or 2000 rupees per month and once you are able to feel the pulse of your achievement in the world of investment, then it is the time for you to keep going your activity to make investment under SIP Plan. The investor in Systematic Investment Plan has not to worry for too fast rise in the market or too fast downfall of the market.

❑❑❑

87

Make Investments as per your Financial Goal

Always think of your financial goal and only then make your investment. Well, the important million dollar question is what should your financial goal be. The answer, however, will depend upon different persons specially depending on their size of the family, their risk profile, their income profile as also what their needs are going to be for next 5, 10 and 20 years. Hence, it is time for every investor to sit down and write down one's financial goals of life and thereafter start backward process of planning of his investments and strategies so as to achieve long term financial goals. One can prepare short term financial goals and also one should prepare long term financial goals which should ultimately end up in planning your strategy for your successful, blissful retirement planning. The money invested by you should be so invested so as to enable you to make your commitments with regard to buying a new car at an appropriate time or buying a house and thereafter providing good education to the children and little later when the children grow up, think of exchanging your house to a big place to live in coupled with your financial obligation to meet the expenses for higher education of the children and finally the expenditure to be made on the marriage of the children. This financial goal of yours for your family finally would come to an end when you prepare the financial goal for your own retirement planning. Plan what you want to achieve at 60 plus age. Plan write now and today what you want your income to be minimum when you are sixty plus. Depending on these goals your aggressive approach will start for the investments which you want to make today.

❑❑❑

88

Deserve versus Desire

The formula of life is deserve versus desire. Well, in the investment scenario also this life formula plays a vital role. One should adopt this formula at every stage of investment planning. You make a particular investment and you desire that the investment should become four fold in five year time. Five years later when you examine the investment, you find that what you have desired has not happened. This reality brings a gloomy face for you. Well, at that point of time you should leave everything to the formula of life namely deserve v. desire. I desire to make my investment grow very fast. This is the wish of every one. But it is God's desire that I deserve not to have so much appreciation in a particular period of time. Hence, if the investment projected and planned by you does not appreciate or bloom to the horizon you are expecting, then always think of this formula of life namely deserve v. desire. Leave everything to the Almighty God because he alone knows what I deserve. But it is my desire which I want to get it fulfilled. Hence, if my desire is not fulfilled in the sphere of investment growth, then one should leave it in the hands of the God and think that it is what you deserve that God has done to your investment. This type of attitude takes away your gloomy face, takes away worries and tensions on the investment front and makes you happy and relaxed. However, from your side definitely you must carry out all those activities which are necessary to make your work get go relating to proper investment strategy implementation.

❑❑❑

89

Yearly Stock Taking of Invisible Funds

At least once a year it is time for you to take a stock of your invisible funds which are under your control and power. Take advantage of the invisible funds at your control and -use those funds for advantage to multiply your money specially when the opportunity arises. For example you might have seen at particular time when the stock market comes at a top bottom. It is this time when one should make investment in the stock market. This is the fact already well-known to every investor. You are in a fix at that point of time because you have no money at your disposal which you can invest to take advantage of the falling stock rates. It is at that point of time you must take advantage of the hidden power of your invisible funds. These invisible funds are in the form of taking loan against your life insurance policy and also taking loan against the Provident Fund and the Public Provident Fund Account maintained by you. Similarly it is this invisible funds which are also locked in the bank Fixed Deposit of yours. Hence, it is time for you now to prepare a chart of invisible funds available at your disposal which can be made available to you within 3 or 7 days time. Once you prepare a chart of your invisible funds, then definitely it helps you to earn more income and more profit at an appropriate time when the opportunity arises. Using invisible funds can help you to make big money at appropriate time if you are able to use these funds for lucrative investment gain. Hence do have regular review of all your assets and more particularly to assets which are in the form of invisible assets but can be used in case of emergency.

❑❑❑

90

Appetite for Taking Risk

Just think before making investment decision. Your risk however, would depend upon your present day assets and liabilities. For example an investor who is having hardly Rs.1 lakh as on today should not venture to take a risk of investing in the stock market. In comparison, a person having 20-50 lakhs of rupees with him in the form of different assets a very few liabilities, then such a person can definitely venture in investment in the stock market and take the risk of making this investment. Therefore, whenever you are planning your investment. Strategy, do take care always to utilize your appetite of taking risk which should be dependent merely on your thinking that yes you are a very daring person and you can take the risk, but this risk appetite should be arrived at by judicious interpretation and thinking and examination of the present day your assets and your liabilities. Never think of becoming a daring personality as far as investments are concerned. The concept of being daring personality of yours should only be dependent upon your strong assets which are under your command. Yes, if you are a person with substantial very good investment in size and value it is only then that you call yourself a daring person to take daring decisions to make investments in the stock market or any other risky investment proposal. On the other hand if you have got quantity of assets but coupled with that you have too big liabilities also, then also it makes a sense to go in a little balanced manner with regard to the investments and not to venture for exposing your daring attitude for investment.

❑❑❑

91

Invest in Kisan Vikas Patra

Kisan Vikas Patra, an investment coming through Post Office also is very lucrative and popular form of investment specially for all those persons who want their investment to be completely safe and secured and are not in need or regular income right at the moment. For all such persons investment is strongly recommended in Kisan Vikas Patra which is available from all the post offices in India.

A new instrument has been issued recently by the Government in terms of the powers enjoyed by the Government under section 12 of the Government Savings Certificate Act, 1959. Whether to invest in the new Kisan Vikas Patra Scheme or not is an important issue for which the decision should be taken by the investor after screening the salient features of this new instrument of investment. Detailed rules and regulations with reference to Kisan Vikas Patra has now been made available by the Government by publication of Kisan Vikas Patra Rules 2014 which have been issued vide Notification No. GSR No. 705(E) dated 23rd September 2014. Before we come to the final conclusion as to whether one should go in for investment in this new Kisan Vikas Patra one should understand carefully the salient features of the Kisan Vikas Patra. Only then the decision should be taken to invest or not to invest in this new Kisan Vikas Patra. It may be noted here that earlier Kisan Vikas Patra were made available since 1988 and later on investment in the Kisan Vikas Patra of 1988 regime were scrapped and that the same was not available for investment. However, the earlier Kisan Vikas Patra provided for higher yield and lower period of holding of Kisan Vikas Patra in comparison with the new rules and regulations to this effect. Hence, please do not compare the erstwhile Kisan Vikas Patra with the new format under which they have been issued. Before we go a step further it will be worthwhile to have a glance of the salient features of the newly launched Kisan Vikas Patra. Here is the list of some of the most important salient features of the Kisan Vikas Patra:-

1. Money invested will become double in eight years and four months. It may be recalled here that earlier under the Kisan Vikas Scheme money would have multiplied only in five and a half years.
2. Interest will come to about 8.7 per cent per annum.
3. KYC norms would not be necessary. The requirement of PAN Card will not be there. However, identification and proof of residence is required to be given.
4. The best feature of Kisan Vikas Patra is safety and security.
5. The HUF and the NRI cannot invest in Kisan Vikas Patra. This Kisan Vikas Patra would be available in the nomination of Rs. 1000, 5000, 10,000, 50,000. However, there is no upper ceiling for investment.
6. Due to decline in the savings rate the new Kisan Vikas Patra has been introduced to provide yet another investment vistas specially for the small and the common man.
7. Kisan Vikas Patra should not be treated as an instrument to plough back the black money.
8. The biggest disadvantage of investment in the Kisan Vikas Patra is it does not enjoy any tax benefit. For

example, the benefit of section 80C is not available and likewise the benefit of interest exemption is not available. The interest will be taxable.

Once having known about the salient features of Kisan Vikas Patra let us screen the different provisions little bit in greater detail so that we can come to the finer points before making investment in Kisan Vikas Patra.

As mentioned above the new Kisan Vikas Patra can be issued in denominations of Rs. 1000, Rs. 5000, Rs. 10000 and Rs. 50000. Besides, any number of certificates of the denominations specified above may be purchased. One can go and purchase these certificates from the Post Office. The Kisan Vikas Patra would be available for sale from any Departmental Post Office in India doing savings bank work.

The Kisan Vikas Patra Certificate may be transferred from one Post Office or bank to any other Post Office or bank after making an application in prescribed Form No. B either at Post Office or at bank.

It is simple to transfer the Kisan Vikas Patra Certificate from one person to another person with the consent in writing to an Officer of the Post Office or bank. Likewise, there are simple rules and procedures for transfer of the certificate to the nominee of the deseased holder.

Likewise, it is specifically provided in these rules that if Kisan Vikas Patra is encashed any time after expiry of two years and six months from the date of its issue, the amount payable inclusive of interest shall be as per the following table:

Table showing premature encashment value of Certificate –

Denomination of Rs. 1,000/-

Table **(Amount in Rs.)**

After (1)	*Amount payable* (2)
2 and half years but less than 3 years	1201
3 years but less than 3 and half years	1246
3 and half years but less than 4 years	1293
4 years but less than 4 and half years	1341
4 and half years but less than 5 years	1391
5 years but less than 5 and half years	1443
5 and half years but less than 6 years	1497
6 years but less than 6 and half years	1553
6 and half years but less than 7 years	1611
7 years but less than 7 and half years	1671
7 and half years but less than 8 years	1733
8 years but before the maturity of the Certificate	1798
On maturity of Certificate	2000

Now having screened the various salient features of the Kisan Vikas Patra now comes the time to take a decision whether you should invest now in Kisan Vikas Patra or not. Generally speaking for tax payers who are coming within the highest income bracket, the investment in Kisan Vikas Patra may not be a profitable investment. However, the best investment of Kisan Vikas Patra will be for all those persons who are having income much below the basic income-tax exemption so that the impact of income-tax is not felt by them at the time of encashment of the Kisan Vikas Patra. This is mainly because of the fact that the yearly interest received by a person making investment in Kisan Vikas Patra is the same and only if together with other income of the individual if it is much below the exemption limit of income-tax, then the question of any tax liability will not arise at all. Reversely, for all those persons who are let us say coming within the 30 per cent tax bracket, for them it may not be a good proposal to think of making investment in Kisan Vikas Patra.

There is no upper ceiling of investment and likewise there is no ceiling that the investment can be made only at one go in one year. Thus, easy investment at your flexible time makes the investment interesting one.

❑❑❑

92

Time to take out Mediclaim Policy

Mediclaim Policy should be taken out but while taking out such Mediclaim Policy special care should be taken to ensure that your major surgical benefits are covered in the said Mediclaim Policy. Sometimes critical illnesses are not covered in the Mediclaim Policy. Therefore, before taking out any Mediclaim, please ensure very specifically from the insurance company that all surgical benefits are available to the policy holder. Before signing the Mediclaim papers, please also have a look at the exclusions which are mentioned in the said Mediclaim Policy. Some of the insurance companies while granting mediclaim policy ask for some extra premium for providing some extra benefit. It is worthwhile to take advantage of extra benefits if they can be made available in the mediclaim policy by making some additional payment of premium. However, it should be noted that major insurance companies granting mediclaim policy exclude the claims arising from pre-existing illnesses.

❑❑❑

93

Use of Surplus Funds

Surplus funds you are having, unable to make the investment in such instruments where the money will be blocked for a long time. Hence, it is important for you now to park your surplus funds at least in Liquid Mutual Funds. If you park the money in the Liquid Mutual Funds, then you are likely to get 3 to 5 per cent yield per annum and moreover such yield becomes tax free for you specially because it is income from Mutual Fund. Hence, all those persons having surplus funds for some short period and they are unable to fix the date of utilization of such funds, then it is definitely a wise decision to park the funds in the Liquid Funds of the Mutual Funds. For example if you have got a grown up daughter, you are looking for a match for her. You are however ready for meeting out .the marriage expenses. You have organized money for the expenditure of marriage of your daughter and it is lying in the bank account. Now so long as the final marriage date is not fixed up, it is wise decision to invest the money in the Liquid Fund of the Mutual Fund. In case you keep the money in the liquid fund then it is easy to get the money in just two days so the money is handy.

❑❑❑

94

Investment in Fixed Maturity Plans

Fixed Maturity Plan (FMP) of the Mutual Fund is a good instrument to enable you to plan your cash flow position. For example some of the Mutual Funds have come out with a fixed maturity plan of 22 months or 26 months. This means that today when you make investment in the said Mutual Fund, you are definitely going to get the redemption amount of the Mutual Fund investment by the said 26 months. The investment in the Fixed Maturity Plan does not bring in very high yield but the advantage is it enables you to plan your cash flow specially when you have got planned commitment of big expenditure which coincides with the date of the Fixed Maturity Plan of a Mutual Fund. Hence, it makes a sense to take advantage of Fixed Maturity Plan of any of the Mutual Funds to plan your guaranteed cash flow requirement in a given situation.

❑❑❑

95

Investment in Sector Based Mutual Funds

As far as possible do not make investment in the Sector Based Funds of a Mutual Fund. The Sector Based Funds have not performed very well in the last couple of years. It is a well known fact that various categories of Mutual Funds instruments are available for an investor. Out of these various varieties of the Mutual Funds, the Sector Funds are the riskiest amongst all such varieties of Mutual Fund. The main reason of their risk is that the investment in these Funds are made only in a particular specific industry or a specific sector. The appreciation or depreciation of the money invested in the said Sector Fund is depending upon the rise or fall of that particular sector or industry in a given time. Hence; it is worthwhile to escape your investment in the Sector Funds.

❑❑❑

96

It is time to Increase Corpus Amount of Investment

Early to bed and early to rise is the way to be healthy, wealthy and wise. This is what we have all learnt from the first class of our school. Now in the field of investment also the same principle would act as an important mantra specially for those who are young and for those who have just started making money either in their service career or in their business or profession. To reap the best fruits of your investment and to enable you to plan your retirement well in advance by your own self, it definitely makes a sense to start invest early. Please therefore increase your investible funds or the corpus amount for investment right from day one when you start earning money. Sometimes it may happen that you are not earning at all. You may be the house wife. No income is going to come to you. But you have inherited some properties or some assets, even in such situation it makes a sense for you to save out of that and start investing wisely. Please do remember it is always good to start early investment. The biggest fruits of early investment by you are going to be reaped by you only. Hence, start your journey into the wonderland of investment right from day one when the income arrives to you.

❑❑❑

97

Pension Plan Investment

Pension Plan, well you may say that you do not need the pension right now. But still for all those who would like to receive regular pension at regular intervals during those golden years which have yet to come, then it is worthwhile to make your investment in the Pension Plan which are being made now available by various insurance companies in India. Don't just go for the yield which these Pension Plans offer. Sometimes the yield which you receive in the Pension Plan does not appear to be lucrative one. Still it makes a sense to go n for Pension Plan to plan your golden years in future. When you are 20, 25, no you may not take Pension Plan, okay no problem. But as you cross the ladder of 35 years of your life, it is time for you now to think and plan and plan and think about various Pension Plans to help you to save for your old age. Do remember that your investment in the Pension Plan also makes available for you a special tax deduction within the overall limit of section 80C etc. Hence, within the limit of Rs.1,50,000 investment you can also make payment for the Pension Plan and enjoy the tax benefit as per a separate section namely section 80CCC of the Income-tax Act, 1961. This Pension Plan Investment mantra is recommended for all those who are within the age group of 35 to 55 in particular. As per the Finance Act, 2015 additional tax deduction on Rs. 50,000 is available on making additional investment in NPS as per section 80CCD (1B) of the Income Tax Act, 1961.

❑❑❑

98

Investments in Hybrid Mutual Funds

You can go in for making investment in the Hybrid Mutual Funds. While you make investment in the Hybrid Mutual Funds, do think that they are the Equity Oriented Mutual Funds. Whenever, the investments are made in these Funds, one should carefully see the assets allocation. This is necessary and essential specially from the point of view of planning of tax on capital gain. The main reason is that if the Hybrid Fund does not contain 65 per cent plus investment in the equity, then it ceases to qualify for all the tax exemptions and benefits available for investment in the Equity Mutual Fund. However, your investment in Hybrid Fund will divide your risk with regard to the investment made by you in the Mutual Fund.

❑❑❑

99

Time to Create Emergency Crisis Fund

Create ECS in your group. Yes, this is an innovative idea of management of your investments whereby you create Emergency Crisis Fund (ECS) for you and your family. Well, the aim of creating Emergency Crisis Fund (ECS) in your family is to ensure that in a given emergency where financial resources are needed, your investments are ready to pull in the required emergency funds to avoid any financial loss or any other loss of any other type. Please remember this type of investment enables you to help in a given emergency period, hence the utility of this investment even if the yield is not that good.

❑❑❑

100

Taking Advantage of Tax-Deduction

In each Financial Year start your investment strategy firstly by making investments which would qualify for tax deduction under the provisions of the Income-tax Law and only thereafter think of making investment in any other vistas or sphere. This should be your first investment strategy. For example for the Financial Year 2015-2016 which started from 1st April 2015 all investors of India as far as possible should try to make the investment in one or more of those items which qualify for tax deduction in terms of section 80C of the Income-tax Act, 1961. The maximum amount on which you can get tax deduction on various investments as per section 80C is Rs. 1,50,000. You can also get additional tax deduction of Rs. 50,000 on your investment in NPS as per section 80CCD (1B) of the income-tax Act. Deduction would be permissible on Medical insurance policy as per section 80D. The sum of Rs. 10,000 being bank interest would also be exempted as per section 80TTA. The main reason is that supposing today you start making your investment right in the beginning of the Financial Year in some other instruments which do not qualify for tax rebate or tax deduction but by the time the Financial Year comes to a close, you find that you are in a fix because you do not have money available at your disposal to make the investment for taking advantage of tax deduction and thereby you may be forced to pay extra income-tax and have extra tax liability for not taking advantage of the provisions of the deductions and exemptions. Hence, do remember always that try to take advantage of making investment in the start of the Financial Year in those instruments which will provide you complete deduction from tax angle.

❑❑❑

101

Nomination Facility for Your Investments

While you discuss and talk and think about the investment strategy, it is worthwhile to take care of important points which relates to protection of your investment for your successors. Hence, do remember to make a nomination facility for all the investments which you have made. However, merely by mentioning the name of nomination in the given investment is not compulsory that in all situations and always the money will go away after your demise to the persons whose names you have nominated. You always have the option to change the nomination as many times as you like. Besides, by preparation of the WILL you can cancel all the nominations because in case a WILL is prepared, the nominations made by you for a particular investment will be superseded by the contents of the WILL. Hence, do plan now to assure that for all the investments there is a nomination or in the alternative a WILL is prepared giving the details of successors to your investment in the years to come. It is also suggested that as far as possible for the safety and security and better management of your investment do take out all the investments in joint names. Hence, it is suggested that please get the names of another family members added with you in most of the investments which you make be it a bank FDR or be it any other investment of this type or be it a Mutual Fund etc.

❑❑❑

102

Guilt Mutual Fund

Guilt funds of various Mutual Funds is again a good investment opportunity being available to all those investors who are most concerned about the safety and security of the investment made by them. The investment which you make in the Guilt Mutual Fund goes to invest finally only in Government Securities and Treasury Bills. It is because of this investment pattern by the Mutual Fund which provides higher safety and security to the investor. However, it will not be correct to expect too heavy returns from your investment in the Guilt Mutual Fund. The Guilt Mutual Fund invests in Government Bonds also Money Market Instruments or some Treasury Bills or Bonds or a combination of one or more of these things. The yield from Guilt Mutual Fund is normally moderate return. From the point of view of protection of the principal amount invested the Guilt Fund of the Mutual Fund provides highest level of safety and security to the investor.

❑❑❑

103

Entry Load of a Mutual Fund

Take care always of the entry load and the exist load which is mentioned in the policy document of the Mutual Fund. Getting in or Getting out of the Mutual Fund is very simple. It is the child's play as it has no hassles and no tension at all. However, the only tension with regard to investment in the Mutual Fund is the tension of Exit Load on the investor as also the tension of entry load on the investor in respect of the investment made by him. Hence, before taking out your investment in the Mutual Fund, it is time for you now to screen very carefully the terms and conditions of a particular Mutual Fund specially with regard to the terms and conditions relating to entry load and exit load.

❑❑❑

104

Systematic Withdrawal Plan

Systematic Withdrawal Plan (SWP) is very close to the concept of Systematic Investment Plan (SIP). Hence, if you are contemplating of withdrawing the money from your Mutual Fund, kindly go through it in greater detail. Specially read out all the rules and regulations of a particular Mutual Fund with regard to Systematic Withdrawal Plan {SWP}. Under this Systematic Withdrawal Plan the Mutual Fund prepares the plan whereby it allows the investor to withdraw the predecided amount from the investment made by him in a particular scheme at a given interval. From the point of view of income-tax planning the Systematic Withdrawal Plan should be prepared keeping in view the tax liability on account of long-term or short term capital gain.

❑❑❑

105

Investment Ratio in Stock Market

Aim higher investment in Equity Market specially when you are very young. For example if you are just 20 plus it is too early for you to start your investment, then surely it is time for you right now and particularly for all those who are within the age group of 20 to 30 years to start investing mainly in the Equity Market and you can keep your total investment portfolio in the Equity Market to as high as 82 per cent to 100 per cent and just remain married to the Equity for a long time but the first thing is do invest now vigorously and specifically when you are very young to start the investment, this is mainly, because you can afford to take higher risk at this point of time. Reversely when you are 50 plus, then it is time for you now to reverse the investment ratio in the stock market. While the young 20 plus should invest 82 per cent as mentioned above in the stock market, the 50 plus investor should invest the reverse amount namely 28 per cent only in the stock market.

❑❑❑

106

Investment in Post Office Savings Account or Money Market Mutual Fund

Shift from keeping money in Savings Bank Account to money in Post Office Savings Bank Account or Money Market Mutual Fund or Liquid Fund so as to have tax free income. If you are sure to keep a particular amount regularly in the Savings Bank Account, instead of that better keep the same money in the Savings Account of a Post Office whereby you are able to enjoy 3.5 per cent tax free income which is payable annually by crediting to your account. The entire income by way of interest from Post Office Savings Bank is completely exempt from income-tax. However, do remember that the minimum amount required for opening the Post Office Savings Bank Account is Rs.50 but the maximum amount which can be kept in the said Savings Bank Account is Rs.1 lakh for individual and Rs.2 lakhs for a joint P.O. Savings Account.

❑❑❑

107

Do not Mortgage your Residential House Property

You may have a good comfortable place to live in. Or you may be the proud owner of a luxurious villa or a mansion where you stay right now. However, in all situations you should never consider your house where you stay as your asset. It is a well known fact that the prices of the real estate have appreciated to unprecedented level, in the last two decades. Hence, you may be staying in any part of India or abroad, but still in most cases the substantial appreciation has taken place in the value of the residential property owned by you where you are residing. However, whatsoever may be the appreciation in the residential property owned by you, but never ever factor your house in the total investments owned by you. This is mainly because of the fact that there might have been appreciation in the value of your house property but the fact remains that we cannot use the appreciated money of the house for our advantage in near future. This is the reality of the situation. Hence, whenever you are planning any investment strategy of your own or you are working out a long-term financial goal for you and your family, do not at any point of time think about the market value of the house where you stay. It is a good investment. It is an investment for emergency.It is an investment to take care of unprecedented future problems if any but this investment in no case should be considered and viewed as your investment. Hence, never ever count the value of this self occupied house property in the total figure of investments owned by you. Also take care to ensure that as far as possible do not mortgage your residential house property either for some temporary loan or for business loan etc.

❑❑❑

108

Beware of Credit Card Insurance

Beware of Credit Card Insurance. You may be having very good limit for your credit card. You are very happy and excited and you feel it as a great status symbol for you. Well, this is the normal thinking of most of the people. Similarly, many times it is seen that the credit card also offers you Insurance Policy. Once such policy is granted to you by a credit card company, you feel happy and relaxed because this insurance has come to you for free. However, please make sure that the Credit Card Insurance policy granted by the credit card company in most cases covers only accidental death and that the natural death which may be caused due to illness of the credit card owner is not at all covered in the said insurance policy issued by the credit card. Therefore, if you are granted an insurance by the credit card company, don't count it as a very good policy to form the part of your total insurance.

❑❑❑